"Don't Despise Our Youth brings a refreshing balance of scholarly research, real-life experiences, and a panoramic look at urban youth ministry and its necessity. Being David A. Washington's youth pastor is one of the greatest gifts of my life and ministry. This book will help readers get a fresh perspective on the transformative power of relevant urban youth ministry. This is a must-read for parents, senior pastors, urban leaders, and those serious about ministry to youth! Great read and needed resource!"

Harvey Carey, founding and senior pastor of Faith Citadel Church

"Don't Despise Our Youth by David A. Washington is a must-read for those seeking to save the next generation of Christ followers and faith leaders. It is one of the most thoughtful and practical books on youth ministry. David Washington has brought years of study and experience to this transformational work of youth ministry. He is the direct product of the power of youth ministry. It saved him and changed the trajectory of his life forever. As you dive into this biblically based work, prepare your heart and mind to be confronted and challenged to save our youth and our future."

D. Darrell Griffin, senior pastor of Oakdale Covenant Church of Chicago and author of *Building a Better You*

"It's never been harder to be a student, and it's even harder in our urban centers where they are confronted with poverty, violence, and drug use. The church is in a unique position to combat these challenges and show our young people a better way. In *Don't Despise Our Youth*, David A. Washington calls attention to this important mission and offers a strategy for how to get it done. This book, drawing on the courage of someone who experienced these challenges firsthand, provides a framework that will allow leaders to reach today's youth, proclaiming God's love in a fractured, hurting world."

Dave Ferguson, founding pastor of Community Christian Church and CEO of Exponential

"David A. Washington is a man of God who lives in the book. I have had the pleasure of walking closely with Pastor David for many years. He is one of the few people who, when I call, you know the odds are he is studying God's Word. Drawing deeply from his own conversion and growth as a teenage believer, David systematically teaches us how to overcome our age bias to make faithful and fruitful disciples of the next generation. Our youth are believers, not babies!"

John Teter, founding pastor of Holy Faith Fellowship and author of the *1-1-1 Finishing Well* newsletter and *The Power of the 72*

DON'T DESPISE OUR YOUTH

RENEWING HOPE FOR URBAN YOUTH MINISTRY

DAVID A. WASHINGTON

ivp

An imprint of InterVarsity Press
Downers Grove, Illinois

InterVarsity Press
P.O. Box 1400 | Downers Grove, IL 60515-1426
ivpress.com | email@ivpress.com

InterVarsity Press® is the publishing division of InterVarsity Christian Fellowship/USA®. For more information, visit intervarsity.org.

All Scripture quotations, unless otherwise indicated, are taken from The Holy Bible, New International Version®, NIV®. Copyright © 1973, 1978, 1984, 2011 by Biblica, Inc.™ Used by permission of Zondervan. All rights reserved worldwide. www.zondervan.com. The "NIV" and "New International Version" are trademarks registered in the United States Patent and Trademark Office by Biblica, Inc.™

While any stories in this book are true, some names and identifying information may have been changed to protect the privacy of individuals.

The publisher cannot verify the accuracy or functionality of website URLs used in this book beyond the date of publication.

Cover design: Faceout Studio, Tim Green
Interior design: Jeanna Wiggins
Images: © Etienne Girardet / fStop, © Colors Hunter - Chasseur de Couleurs / Moment,
        via Getty Images

ISBN 978-1-5140-1302-1 (print) | ISBN 978-1-5140-1303-8 (digital)

Printed in the United States of America ∞

Library of Congress Cataloging-in-Publication Data
A catalog record for this book is available from the Library of Congress.

31 30 29 28 27 26 25 | 12 11 10 9 8 7 6 5 4 3 2 1

TO PASTOR HARVEY F. CAREY,

my mentor, spiritual father, and leader, who continues

to be a model and support for the work God has called me to.

Your ministry saved and changed my life,

for which I am eternally grateful.

———————

TO MY PARENTS, MYRTIS LEE AND DAVID CHARLES,

for never giving up on me, praying for me,

and sacrificing so much to rescue me from the grips

of the Chicago streets. Words will never be sufficient to convey

the gratitude for the parents God placed in my life.

———————

TO MY WIFE, VERNÉE,

AND CHILDREN, DAVID AND CHEMIN,

thanks for your support and patience in the journey of life and ministry.

Thanks for being an inspiration to me during both the good

and dark times on this road of kingdom building!

CONTENTS

1

A CULTURAL DISCLAIMER

CULTURE AND CONTEXT ARE extremely important factors for consideration in ministry. These ideals are meant to guide our understanding of how to carry out ministry in our churches. Sometimes culture can be shocking and difficult to receive by those on the outside of the particular culture, but as God calls us to serve in particular contexts, awareness of those cultural contexts is an important part of that work.

In this book, I will be addressing issues that are deeply cultural and contextual to life and ministry in urban low-income and African American communities and its impact on adolescents living within them. Most of what I will share will narrow in on my personal experience and is not meant to give an exhaustive look at the elements of urban and African American life. Although much of the content will address some of the darkest issues in these communities, it is important to understand that this is not a full and complete picture of Black communities.

Some of the content of this book may be disturbing and seemingly too graphic, but for those serving churches in urban poor communities, it paints a realistic picture of the tough challenges people face on a regular basis. The majority of mainstream resources for youth ministry have avoided vivid descriptions of some of the dark issues faced in urban poor communities. Perhaps this is because most of the books written are not seeing and experiencing what those in this context are. But many serving in this context are experiencing very dark situations and need to know that there is hope for navigating them. The stories in this book are all real and true, and youth workers across the United States are dealing with similar scenarios all the time. Therefore, my aim is to press into the uncharted waters to give hope and help youth workers to understand and navigate the ministry to which God has called them.

This work will focus on some of the prevalent elements of urban inner-city culture such as extreme promiscuity, drug abuse, gang activities, crime, and poverty, that often create inhumane acts of desperation for survival. Issues like these are not easy to address in a Christian book, but the reality is there are countless teenage believers facing all of this and more in their communities. This is the very reason why troubling issues like these should be addressed in Christian books. Often the cordiality and niceness of American Christian culture clashes with the realness of God's work and our Christian witness in the rest of the world. Issues such as drugs, violence, sex, and real-life stories of struggle will get a lot of attention in the pages to follow.

However, I want to be very clear again, that these are not the only elements in our urban communities. There are many productive families with structure and youth who operate in academic excellence; youth who are gifted artistically, academically, and in service. Community businesses that are owned by families in the community and countless organizations provide opportunities for families to thrive in the community. Many of the youth operating in these situations are not as difficult to shepherd as others. Because youth workers in the urban poor setting are also dealing with teenagers who are wrestling with issues of intense challenge, the majority of this book will share relevant stories of transformation and discuss factors germane to some of the darkest issues that youth workers have to engage. Youth workers are more in need of hope and guidance in serving youth who are functioning in the darkest places than those who are on the right track, though these youth have their struggles as well.

I also want to be clear that many of the challenging issues addressed in this work also affect White, suburban, and rural contexts and will hopefully be helpful to practitioners beyond the urban setting. Although they may manifest in different ways in the suburbs or countryside, I believe the way they are addressed in this book would be helpful to the other contexts as well. Young people in the United States are dealing with disastrous issues that we need to be equipped to assist them with.

Furthermore, our silence is not of assistance to them. I was raised in an impoverished, violent, and harsh environment just like countless other youth today. There are unique challenges in this context that need to be noted and addressed vividly. Not only was I raised in such a dark culture, but I have done ministry with youth within this culture for over thirty years.

There are many congregations and youth ministers serving on the front lines of inner-city conflict and trauma. These populations have been referred to as "traumatrigenic" communities. That is descriptive of the community's state of "living with constant pressure of violence, poverty, drugs, death, and powerlessness as a daily walk of life."[1] There are youth ministers in need of help to address the unique challenges that many resources on youth ministry fail to understand and are ill equipped to handle. For this reason, the transparency and descriptive dialogue in this work is necessary. This book at times goes in depth to highlight urban contextual issues because teenagers are heavily engaged in or exposed to them in major cities around the country.

One prevalent issue in urban youth ministry is drug abuse and drug dealing. Drugs are a part of the culture of youth in low-income and urban Black communities. The average youth pastor in this context serves multiple youth who are addicted to alcohol, drugs, and illegal sources of income. There are youth who struggle with low self-esteem due to the perceived struggle associated with escaping their environment. Drug and alcohol addiction, along with racial discrimination and the effects of White supremacy and systemic racism, affects how many of these teenagers see their worth as well. Poverty is a real issue. There are teens dealing with homelessness, parents on drugs, and the feeling of having to be on the wrong side of the law in order to survive.

Another prevalent issue in urban youth ministry is gangs. Many young men and women are frequently falling victim to gang affiliation, violence, and death. Gang members and territories surround churches in the inner city. Many of the teenagers in our congregations are members of these gangs or strongly considering it. Only those who have been authentic gang members know what it is really like to be a part of a gang. Those on the outside only see the glitz and glamor, never knowing the whole story until they are in too deep. This is why it is helpful to paint the real picture to help deter other young people who are considering taking that route.

Although this book provides a vivid description of life for communities of color and the experience of low-income areas, it is also useful for churches and youth ministries outside of the urban inner-city context. There is overlap from some of the urban issues that affect areas outside of the inner city. So much of what is suggested to address them will be useful for all distinct ministry contexts who are dealing with these challenges. Also, the biblical principles are practical to utilize for any church, youth leader, parent, or person who works with youth.

However, one important reason to use this book as a resource is to help those who feel called to serve in the urban low-income context to grasp a picture of what it is like along with timeless principles that can be helpful to that work. Many suburban churches that border inner-city areas may feel ill equipped to do ministry in these areas, but this book makes it clear that ministry in the hood is not about color but culture. Just as these churches outside of the Black community can do mission in foreign areas, their help, resources, prayer, and work can benefit the kingdom of God in urban communities and build relationships and comradery with other ministries that may not ethnically and/or culturally look like theirs. Hopefully, this work will be an encouragement for suburban and rural ministries to join God's mission in the inner city.

To be genuine and paint a realistic picture of what youth of color are feeling and facing throughout the inner cities of the United States, I will be sharing real-life stories about my personal seasons of life as a youth. From my experiences as a youth on the streets of Chicago to becoming a youth participating in ministry to my years of service as an urban youth pastor and ultimately a lead pastor of a local church in the inner city of Chicago, the difference maker was the church. The stories of youth I have served over the years and examples of the impact of youth ministry are all key to helping the church see and value youth ministry in our congregations. I will endeavor to provide authentic verifiable truth from the culture for the readers.

This means I will mention some people and characters I had experiences with by name, but for the safety and security of some, I will use aliases. Gangs will be mentioned by their real names and sometimes by their street sets or territories. This is necessary for those serving within this culture to have verifiable details to give credibility to the storyteller and is better received by those functioning within the context. We overcome Satan by the blood of Christ but also by the word of our testimony. If God can deliver young people from heavy addiction, gang involvement, crime, and promiscuous lifestyles, then young people who are struggling with these addictions can find hope for themselves by hearing these real-life stories.

I ask of the reader not to come to quick judgment about the aim of these personal stories and endeavor to see the depths to which God delivers young people from the power of sin. Please understand that the real-life stories and issues described in this work are but a raw reflection of the lives that many teenagers are living in our inner cities. Those who have been able to overcome it are doing the youth of today a disservice by concealing their testimonies and depriving youth of knowing the miracles God has done. Youth on drugs need to know that God can deliver them, youth in gangs need to know that God can bring them out safely, youth struggling to live for God need to know that they can have swag and still love and serve God.

Most importantly for me, I want to make it clear to the readers that I do not share these intimate and vividly detailed stories for any glory or attention to myself, but because there are youth and youth leaders whose attention I would like to draw to the hope found in Christ alone. Regardless of how despondent their situations may seem, God is the author and finisher of our faith. My aim is to help you read this from a real-life perspective and see God's power to address your real-life situations.

2

LIFE OR DEATH CIRCUMSTANCES

Then our sons in their youth will be like well-nurtured plants, and our daughters will be like pillars carved to adorn a palace.

PSALM 144:12

I WAS HIDING IN THE BASEMENT of a storefront building, along with my ride-or-die partner Besko (RIP). We had just gotten into an altercation at a party with some opposing gangsters who drew guns on us. We broke away and ran down a stairway in the back with no idea where we were going. Looking up at the top of the stairs, we saw the silhouette of the three men with guns attempting to murder us. They were walking hesitantly as they did not know the layout of the building or where it would lead them.

All of a sudden, they stopped and looked directly at us from the top of the stairs, but the darkness made it impossible to see us. It is probably the scariest event I have ever experienced. We were looking each other in the eyes, but while we could see them they could not see us. Two of the men were known killers in our neighborhood whose names I will not mention, one of whom was just released from prison after doing five years for a juvenile murder. The basement was so pitch black dark that we couldn't even see our hands in front of our eyes, much less anything else around us. If we bumped into anything, we knew they would hear us and begin firing in our direction. As hard as it was, we stood still not knowing if they could see us, and eventually, they turned around and left the building.

We seized that window of escape, ran into the house upstairs, kicked down the locked door on a family who was smoking crack cocaine, and pushed our way through their front door to escape and save our lives. The next day when we sobered up, we laughed about our narrow escape and kept moving with our day. This was the kind of life we lived every single day back then. It was just another day in the hood for us. We learned to live and function in drama, trauma, and chaos so much that it became normal. Every single day, we did something that could put us in prison or the graveyard. We were teenage gang bangers with no sense of purpose or direction for our lives.

This is a current epidemic in the city of Chicago where gang banging has permeated urban culture, and the distress it causes goes for the most part unmentioned or addressed. Yet, by the grace of God, today I am a Christian and a pastor all because I was introduced to the gospel of Jesus Christ and discipled into maturity as a young man. My transformation did not happen overnight. It happened through constant and persistent ministry from a local church that had unknowingly moved into our community in the middle of a war zone.

We jumped people on the premises and inside the church premises. We had shootouts right outside of their church and even shot up a car full of enemies right in front of their pastor. Crisis like this is still prevalent today and even more abundant in the Chicagoland area, but the gospel of Christ is still powerful enough to reach youth struggling with the wiles of urban life. Urban youth ministry is designed to focus on the deliverance of youth from the challenges of the world as they experience it.

THE STATE OF URBAN YOUTH MINISTRY

I'm sure many urban-centered pastors today would agree that one of the most challenging ministries in the church is youth ministry. Churches are struggling with the turnover rate of youth pastors. They wrestle with hiring someone who will stick with the youth for the long haul. Pastors are constantly hearing complaints from people in the congregation asking, "What are we going to do about the youth?" Most of the time those doing the complaining will not volunteer any time to work with the youth themselves, and the few who do volunteer are often not the right candidates with a heart for young people. This is why a significant amount of traditional Black churches do not have a youth ministry or a full-time youth pastor.

I currently serve as the senior pastor of Kingdom Covenant Church Chicago on the far south side of the city of Chicago. We are serving a traumatrigenic community in the heart of an area where young people are experiencing challenges that are drawing negative national attention to our city. Among these issues are youth violence, crash-and-grab thefts, and riotous takeovers where youth gather by the hundreds in areas downtown, stopping traffic, randomly beating people up, robbing people, and destroying cars and property. The drug epidemic among youth in the city of Chicago is also bringing national attention to the city. Opioid addiction, drinking "lean" (over-the-counter codeine), ecstasy pills, and more are causing overdose and deaths in mass numbers. Kingdom is a multi-generational church, but the young demographic in our congregation needs significant attention.

I have also noticed in multiple seminaries throughout the city that the most requested need in church hires is for youth pastors. The employment opportunity walls in Bible colleges and seminaries across the city are filled with churches requesting applicants for youth ministry positions. Not only are youth workers leaving youth ministry but youth themselves are leaving the church.

Since entering the 2000s, research has shown a decline in church attendance among young adults who attended church as youth. It is stated in "*Youthworker Journal,* according to Lifeway Research, 70 percent of young people will drop out of church after high school, and only 35 percent will return to regular attendance."[1] In 2023 we saw:

> The next generation is often leaving the faith while under the supervision of parents who believe they're passing on their religious values. In the early 1990s, no more than 16% of 8th, 10th, and 12th graders said religion was not important to them at all, according to the Monitoring the Future survey series. By the early 2000s, however, the percentage of high school seniors who completely dismissed the importance of religion to them personally began to increase dramatically.[2]

Why are so many churches struggling to find and keep youth pastors? Why are so many youth pastors leaving their positions so quickly and frequently? Why are so many young people leaving the church? Why are so many former teens failing to find a place to fit in the adult ministry of the church after going through youth ministry? I am not sure about the answer to each of these questions, but I believe they are all connected to one thing: youth ministry today is not held to the value it deserves. I believe that many urban churches are despising youth and youth ministry, which is perpetuating the crisis that exists among urban youth today.

THE YOUTH MINISTRY CRISIS

I agree with many that there is a youth crisis of epidemic proportions, but I also believe the youth crisis is a symptom of the decline of youth ministry. There is a distinction between a youth crisis and a youth ministry crisis. Our contemporary youth crisis is about the catastrophe of the growing trauma and chaos youth are exposed to and affected by. Mass shootings, gang violence, hard illegal drugs, opioid addictions, overdoses, the victimization of young people to urban crimes, and prison recidivism are but a few of the issues for urban youth. These challenges create and contribute to their trauma and chaotic environment. In the past, many teens have found ways to live above the chaos and transcend the trauma. One of those channels supporting them was their local churches' youth ministry.

I am a living witness that a strong youth ministry is able to infiltrate the chaotic setting that youth in urban America live in. Youth ministry can liberate them from its traumatic impact on their lives. I know this because I was one of those youth and my life was forever transformed by the power of youth ministry. Through youth workers who treasured teenagers and valued the work of youth ministry, my life was invested in and

I received the guidance I needed. I grew up on the far south side of Chicago in the Roseland and Pullman communities, an area known on the streets and around the world as the Wild Wild Hundreds. This area is called wild because of the urban chaos that is perpetuated here. But churches in this area engaged the community, reached out, and raised youth in their churches, providing free and affordable resources to help youth get through their struggles without permanent mental and emotional damage.

Research suggests that only 7 percent of youth pastors stay in their position for more than seven years.[3] I have experienced that in the average urban African American church that has a youth ministry, most youth pastors stay no longer than three years. It seems that youth ministers are more likely to look at their assignment as a necessary step to another coveted position rather than a serious call to raise up the next generation of the church. Our youth are in desperate need of churches and their leaders to understand the importance of youth ministry to end this crisis. But before we can value the need for robust youth ministry, we need to recognize how the existing crisis in urban youth ministry came to be.

THE GROWTH OF URBAN YOUTH MINISTRY

Youth ministry at one point in time was strong in cities across the country, but then there was a decline. The internal work of the church to develop young disciples is not the only struggle. The external work of the church to reach youth in the community is a struggle as well. There is a larger demographic of unchurched youth growing up in the urban context who are indifferent to the church, impressionable, and without a sense of direction and purpose. There is an immense population of youth who did not grow up in church and are totally oblivious to worship, God, and the Bible.

In my experience these young people are easier to raise up as disciples of Christ than many of the teens being raised in the church, and they are more impactful in strengthening the faith of the youth who are the so called "church kids." Perhaps this is because many young people growing up in the church are struggling with feeling alienated from their peers and desiring to fit in with those outside of the church. Some fall into the temptation of trying to identify with their unchurched peers and others backslide but continue to attend church out of family duty without real personal spiritual transformation.

I feel like these so called church kids may struggle with the shame of the stigma as well as familiarity with church, so discipleship often begins with working through some of the trouble and church hurts they have experienced and finding inspiration from other Christian youth living a faithful life in Christ. Finding a model in young people who have a good balance of faith maturity and teenage swagger is helpful to the discipleship process with youth growing up in the church. Sheep make sheep, which means that young Christians are helpful in making and developing more young Christians. This is why my philosophy and understanding of youth ministry is youth doing ministry.

Youth ministry must be more than adults ministering to youth; it has to be youth doing ministry. So called youth ministries that focus only on ministering to youth may be missing a fundamental game changer: instead of ministering to youth, raise up your youth to minister to each other. I will dive into this concept a bit more in chapter four, because youth ministry can be more effective when it is understood not as ministering to youth but as youth doing ministry.

Formal youth ministry, as we refer to it today, began to develop in the mid-twentieth century as parachurch organizations addressing the needs of youth in society.[4] Youth ministry from its inception was about addressing youth in society and not just the church. The success of organizations like Child Evangelism Fellowship (established 1937), Youth for Christ (established 1944), and Young Life (established 1941) brought attention to addressing the needs of youth while also revealing the power emanating from youth who are being discipled and nurtured in their faith. This attention would eventually cause local churches to begin their own congregational youth ministries and hire pastors to address the needs of youth full-time.

Instrumental and common among our contemporary youth ministries were youth church. Youth church is an entire Sunday worship service designed for youth and attended by youth typically every Sunday but sometimes twice per month, on fifth Sundays, or another Sunday of the church's choosing. At youth church, teenagers would have church together and receive and participate in the worship service with their peers. This helped tremendously with the transformation of youth who were used to being in adult services that seemed to ignore them and address nothing applicable to the youth.

While youth ministry began to be a thing in many White evangelical churches across America in the 1960s and 1970s, urban African American churches did not begin to develop traditional youth ministries as a discipleship focus until after the Civil Rights Movement.[5] Prior to this, youth were trained in prophetic ministry and active resistance to social injustice. Black churches, at the forefront of the Civil Rights Movement, used youth to speak truth to the powers that were. From protests like those held by the youth in Birmingham, Alabama, marches and sit-ins at segregated establishments, youth ministry addressed the world that youth lived and functioned in at the time.

Youth ministries began to shift after the Civil Rights Movement and became strong in the mid-1980s through the late-1990s as the focus of discipleship broadened to include urban African American.[6] This season was followed by an expansion of more church youth ministries, and by the early 2000s youth ministry was a normal thing in both mega and the average local Black church. However, sometime between then and now we have experienced a decline. These modern churches are no less gifted than the earlier churches. Rather, the decline has come in the focus of youth doing ministry, the amount of people committing to serve youth, and their longevity to the service of youth which seems to suggest a need for churches to understand the important value of youth ministry. Therefore, the question is: What caused the decline?

THE DECLINE OF URBAN YOUTH MINISTRY

I want to briefly share some of the ways popular youth ministry has declined since we entered the 2000s. As youth ministry came to be a popular trend among churches, youth for the first time were able to worship among their peers and hear messages that addressed issues that were relevant to them. It was an amazing shift, but as time went on and youth ministry became popular, familiarity with youth church brought about a desensitizing to some of the spiritual focuses. It seemed to become more about having youth in church than raising up Christian disciples. This is why I believe that doing youth ministry alone is not enough. What I mean is that just because a church has a youth ministry doesn't mean it is effectively maturing youth spiritually. Our objective needs to be evangelizing and discipling youth into maturity and empowerment for ministry. With this being the objective in our ministries, it will dictate what we focus on doing. Being able to say we have a youth ministry is one thing, but we should also be able to say we are developing mature Christian youth.

Youth ministries that do not lose sight of their purpose to disciple and raise up strong young followers of Christ is important. As churches began developing youth ministries, particularly youth churches, youth were beginning to be separated from their adult congregations and the senior pastor of the church.[7] This perpetuated an arrested development of sorts among youth. The disconnect with the rest of the church and a sense of siloed independence would affect the ability of these teenagers to integrate with the adult congregation. Teenagers in church were growing in age but unable to find their footing in the adult ministries and worship services of the church as they transitioned into adulthood. Many of these same teens began to slowly backslide when they entered college and their adult years.

Another issue of decline in youth ministries was that just like many adult ministries—it became more entertainment focused than transformation focused. Youth workers focused on youth having fun more than youth growing spiritually. After years of young people having to experience church catered to an older generation, they were now able to do things in church that they were not allowed to before. The things that kept many young people away from church in the past were no longer an issue. Youth could now dance, rap in the church, dress in hip-hop fashion, and have concerts and artful services without any issue. However, for many of these ministries the problem became that they began to focus more on what entertained the youth, perhaps to draw them in from the streets, than what was actually needed to transform their lives into mature Christians.

Another issue causing decline was the church's drive to compete with the world's influences on their young people. The development of music videos, MTV (music television), urban tv shows like *TRL* (*Total Request Live*) or *106 & Park*, even competition with the internet and technology. The church sought to reduplicate, or "redeem," what the world was using in order to reach the youth for God. Unfortunately, this exposes the failure of churches to be creative. Rather than looking at the world to create alternative events, activities, and ministries, we need to be allowing our youth to come up with creative ways to reach their generation without always having to borrow ideas from the world. The church can't compete with the world when it comes to what the world does.

The church cannot compete with sin. We cannot give the youth an alternative to rappers like Kendrick Lamar, Da Baby, ASAP Rocky, or Drake. The youth would always reject the fake Kendrick Lamar for the real one. But while the church can't compete with sin in the world, the world cannot compete with what the church does. The anointing and power of God is unmatched in the world. Worldly icons like Drake can appeal to the flesh of young people, but they cannot compete with the church's ability to connect the spirit and soul of young people to their Creator.

The presence of God is unlike anything the world can produce or offer, and when we create an atmosphere for young people to experience the presence of God, there is nothing in the unchurched world that can match it. Young people need to be in spaces where they can enter God's presence. It comes only from

the church and authentically seeking God. If we are going to
reverse this decline of robust worship for youth, we must first
understand the importance of God's presence and the procla-
mation of his Word in all that we offer youth in our congregations. Once the importance of youth ministry is understood and
the potential and viability of youth in ministry is perceived,
youth ministry will become invested in and effective for the
entire church and its surrounding community.

RESTORING THE VALUE OF URBAN YOUTH MINISTRY

To despise the youth is to undervalue them, their contributions,
and their potential in the ministry of the church. If we are going
to nurture and develop mature Christian youth, we need committed youth workers to understand their value and persevere
in the work. To find these workers, we must restore the value of
urban youth ministry in the culture of our congregations.

The beginning of this introduction provides a quote from
Psalm 144 where King David offers a prayer for the youth, de-
claring that their sons be like well-nurtured plants and their
daughters like pillars carved to adorn a palace. This prayer is a
request for young men to become mature and well-nurtured
like plants or strong trees planted by water streams. In order for
this to happen, our young men must be nurtured, directed, and
developed by older or more mature people, especially those
who have been where they currently are. Youth ministry must
be concerned about the nurturing of young men into who God
has created and called them to be.

David's prayer is also a request for young women to be like
carved pillars of a palace. This prayer is not about natural beauty,
nor does it suggest that our young women become merely ob-
jects of physical attraction. The key to understanding what

David is praying is seen in the phrase "carved to adorn a palace." David is praying that the young women are stable and create stability, that young ladies become like the cornerstone of a palace holding it up and keeping it steady and stable. It is also my prayer that as you read this book, you would recognize the importance of pouring into young people, valuing them, their potential, and their contributions, while recognizing the power of what our young men and women can become to contribute to the church and society as a whole.

Youth who are despised are youth who will be neglected. For some reason, youth ministry is being seen by young adults as illegitimate or baby ministry, which is not what they perceive as the real church. This is an egregious mindset and must be corrected. Youth are the future of the church and always will be. Their future contributions will keep the church thriving, and many times their presence will lead to the presence of their parents and other family members coming to church. Youth are no less valuable than adults. Youth can do just as much and sometimes even more than adults are doing in the kingdom of God. Our youth need for the church as a whole to highly value ministry to and through them.

A BRIEF WALK THROUGH

This book was developed into three parts with chapters to help us understand the need for the particular values that will help us to strengthen youth ministry. The first part of this book is "The Necessity of Worth," which expresses the important need to see the value and worth in youth and youth ministry. In this section, chapter three addresses the subtle ways youth are becoming undervalued in many congregations and offers motivations for focusing on Christian work among the youth. Chapter four offers a working definition for youth ministry that will help establish a means of measuring its success. Chapter five is a reminder to see the value of youth as contributing believers and not as babies who are limited in their service because of their age.

The next part of this book is "The Necessity of Word," which expresses the need to have a biblical basis and theological focus in the work of youth ministry. The Word of God is a necessity in youth ministry, and if we are focused on helping young people grow into who they are called to be, it can only happen through the relentless work of sharing God's Word with them. It is necessary to share, teach, and learn God's Word to develop healthy, robust youth ministries that are respected and supported in our congregations.

This section opens with chapter six, which addresses the necessity of evangelism and witnessing through the Word of God to and through youth. Chapter seven lays out the importance of developing a community of discipleship for youth, young Christians, and youth workers. Discipleship aims to increase spiritual maturity for those who have placed their faith in Christ. Chapter eight points out the necessity of communicating love to the youth, which requires understanding how love is conveyed and experienced by the youth in our care. We must not underestimate the power of God's voice speaking to and through our youth as a result of the ways that they are loved by our churches.

The final section of this book is "The Necessity of War," which discusses the need to fight with and for the youth under our care. Youth ministry workers must understand that war for youth ministry is necessary. Some things will not happen without a fight. Some things you will have to battle for because some of the work will inevitably encounter opposition. This section has two chapters addressing the need for the church to protect and defend the youth. Chapter nine provides inspiration and direction to the various factions of lay people in the congregation on how to best recognize and support the efforts of youth ministry. Chapter ten is addressed to the clergy serving the church and the frequent need to battle for the requirements of the younger generations.

I would encourage you to pray as you dive into each chapter, that God would provide direction for the work that you do to benefit young people. I know that there exists an enormous demand to restore the value of committed continual and faithful kingdom work within the generations of urban youth. Youth becoming stronger in their faith and faith walk with Jesus ought to be an aim in all youth ministries. With this focus as our measuring rod for success, the crisis of youth ministry becomes clearer. The importance of youth ministry is better understood and consequently more valuable.

When we begin to ask not whether we are accumulating more youth but are we developing more young faithful disciples, then we can focus on faithful youth ministry that brings spiritual transformation rather than social amusement. This is a call for the body of Christ to raise the bar, value ministry to and through the youth, and help our young people navigate and decrease the chaos they are experiencing. But before anyone can be motivated to do this, it is necessary to understand the value and worth of youth and youth ministry.

PART ONE

THE NECESSITY OF WORTH

3

DON'T DESPISE
OUR YOUTH

*He looked David over and saw that he was
little more than a boy, glowing with health
and handsome, and he despised him.*

1 SAMUEL 17:42

ONE SUMMER AT THE AGE OF SEVENTEEN, I was holding
the rank of the first chief of the Gangster Disciples Nation on
119th Street. I was traveling with about twelve of my guys on
Indiana Avenue passing 118th Street to retaliate against a rival
gang for jumping one of our guys. That's when I saw for the first
time a man who would soon become known to me as Rev. Harvey
F. Carey. He was the youth pastor of the Salem Baptist Church of
Chicago, which had just purchased a church building in our
community a few months earlier. Recognizing the fire in our eyes,
Pastor Carey did something unexpected. He stepped in front of
us, intentionally interrupting us from our pressing business, to

introduce himself as the youth pastor of this new church. He then asked me my name, to which I replied with my street name, Boonie G. Unsatisfied. With my response, he asked for my government name, and for some reason, I actually told him.

I usually never gave out my real name. I didn't even carry my ID so that I could lie about my identity if I ever got into trouble with the law. This is one of the reasons gang members go by nicknames, aliases, and street monikers. A street name helps to build your reputation and credibility in the neighborhood, so we carefully choose names that will highlight our street personage. The youth pastor said to me, "You have a biblical name. Do you know who King David was in the Bible?" But I abruptly interrupted and said I had to leave. Needless to say, we went about handling our business that day, and I gave it no more thought. However, about three months later I was walking past this church and this youth pastor standing outside again said, "How are you doing, David?" I couldn't believe it. How could he remember my name? I only met him one time months ago.

This encounter would have an indescribable impact on my life. I could not believe that this guy had remembered me by my name after so much time. In hindsight, subconsciously, I must have felt valued. I saw this man one time in the early summer and had not seen him since, but he remembered me. This began our relationship at a time when I was lost and void of direction. The reason this youth pastor remembered my name is because he valued young people. Pastor Carey valued youth ministry and prided himself on helping youth to understand not only who they were but also why they were here. I was not the only young person being reached in the community. Many youths from the neighborhood were invited and started attending the youth church services at Salem Baptist Church of Chicago.

Little did I know some three years later, God would use years of my youth ministry encounters with this church to rescue me from the streets, and I would become a part of this ministry as well.

The sum of it all is that I was able to become who I have become today because a youth pastor looked beyond a lost teenage gangster in the hood and saw in me the great potential to be a soldier in God's army. I was greatly valued by a pastor who focused not on what I had become in the world but on what I had the potential to become in the kingdom of God. When Christians fail to value the spiritual potential of young people, youth become overlooked and disregarded by the church, leaving them more vulnerable to be drawn into the adverse influences of their world. Dope dealers, gangsters, and others looking to exploit them have no problem with giving them that attention and utilizing them in the wrong ways, and these are among the countless giants they are facing on the regular.

THE YOUTH ARE FACING GIANTS

Young people today are facing huge challenges. Violence is claiming the lives of youth throughout urban America. Poverty is causing teenagers to make poor choices that are detrimental to their health, life, and freedom. Popular culture is doing a lot to keep youth focused on making choices that bring immediate gratification but usually lead to future devastation. There are also giants that our young people are facing in our very churches. They are up against the giants of church programming that ignore them and their true spiritual needs. They face the giants of non-committed youth workers and the giants of youth pastors who come in for a couple of years and then leave for a perceived better position abandoning the youth to fend for themselves. Youth in our congregations are facing the giant of adult workers who are unable to see them as viable contributors to the church and treat them like babies rather than servants of God.

Until we understand the power available through the lives of mature and discipled teenagers in our churches, we will continue to miss out on incredible opportunities to do greater works for God. Embracing the value and worth of the youth entrusted to us is critical to building strong youth ministries. When the worth of youth is recognized, young people in the church are less likely to feel undervalued, less important, or despised. I do not mean that churches dislike young people and want nothing to do with them. The word translated "despise" in certain passages like 1 Timothy 4:12 is from the Greek word *kataphroneō*, which "can mean to look down on, or to consider something not important enough to give attention to"—in other words, "to not give esteem to, to disregard or think little or nothing of."[1]

Too often youth in our churches are not esteemed highly enough. I believe youth and youth ministry need more respect, reverence, and expectation to help it contribute to the ministry of the local church. If you see youth in your church as incapable of contributing to your spiritual life, you are despising them. If you don't see youth as qualified to be great teachers and evangelists in the church, you are despising them. If you see youth in your church as babies who need to obey you but cannot lead you, then you are despising them. God can and God does use whoever he chooses. Many churches must change their perspective on young Christians because they are fearfully and wonderfully made to help our churches get to the next level and lead the next generations of our congregations.

28

DESPISED BY MANY

In 1 Samuel 17, we see a young person being underestimated not only in the world but also among the people of God. In this chapter, David is a youth sent by his father to bring lunch to his brothers who are stationed at the battlefield on the front lines of a war with the Philistines. The first to underestimate and despise David is his own father, Jesse, who did not allow him to be on the battlefield or recognize his ability to contribute to the efforts of the war. David was the youngest of all Jesse's sons and was minimized presumably because of his youth. When the prophet Samuel was sent to Jesse's house to anoint the next king of Israel among his sons, Jesse did not even invite David into the room to be considered. How often are our teenagers not even considered as candidates to do mighty works for God? Many church leaders are unable to understand the contributions young people can bring to the ministry and sadly fail to see that they ought to be valued as vessels God can use. Youth like David are frequently despised by many, but they are never despised by God.

Not only was the ministry of David despised by his father, but next we see David is despised by his brother as well. In 1 Samuel 17:28, David's oldest brother Eliab became angry with him and despised his presence near the battlefield. But while Eliab only saw a youth he perceived as being a nosey little brother, God saw a young warrior who had a heart that was more than capable of facing the giant who the rest of God's people were afraid to approach. In the next verses, all the people on the battlefield despised David's presence, and then Saul, the king of Israel, also counted David out simply because he was a youth. When David dared to face a giant who the older soldiers were afraid to face, Saul said to him, "You are not able to go out against this Philistine and fight him; you are only a young man, and he has been a warrior from his youth" (1 Samuel 17:33). If Goliath had been a man of war since his youth, he once was a warrior as a youth. Unfortunately, the people of God failed to value the contributions a young David could make.

Lastly, we see that David was not only despised by God's people he was also despised by the enemy. When he finally went out to fight the Philistine giant, the Scripture says that when the Philistine Goliath "looked David over and saw that he was little more than a boy, glowing with health and handsome . . . he despised him" (1 Samuel 17:42). Simply because he was young, David was underestimated among the congregation of God's people and the enemy they faced. Being despised by the world is understandable, but young people certainly should not be despised by the people of God.

The good news is that despite being despised on every side, David proved all the naysayers wrong. David was young, but what everyone failed to see is that he was a young man who knew God and understood his potential through God. David defeated the giant and changed how he was perceived by everyone. Like young David, most young people just need the opportunity to prove their potential. There are some giants in the church that our youth are equipped to face that many adults in the congregation are not able to face.

Who will God most likely use in the church to minister to the young gangsters? Youth are designed for it, but they just need to be equipped for it. Some young people can get into places that leave many of us cowering on the fringes of the battlefield like the army of Israel. There are giants to be faced that God is raising younger people in our churches to vanquish. A young David helped the people of God see the power of his youthfulness utilized in the hands of God. Many of our churches need to change the negative perspectives of youth in the congregation so that we can empower them to be who God has created them to be. For this we need a revisioning of the youth God has brought into our care.

A NEW LOOK AT THE YOUTH

Our perspective of young people is very important. Proverbs teaches us to "start children off on the way they should go and even when they are old they will not turn from it" (Proverbs 22:6). Training young people helps to secure where they wind up. We are not responsible for babysitting teenagers or facilitating social gatherings for the youth, but training up youth to contribute to God's work in the kingdom. This happens when we can see youth as tools in God's hands rather than babies who need something to do while the adults worship. It will be helpful in gathering more people to work with youth when we look at youth as the young future leaders of the church and can see them as God's vessels.

There is tremendous power in a look. How we see often determines how we think, feel, and behave. If we look at young people as hoodlums and challenges, then we will begin to fear them and create a distance between them and ourselves, treating them as a problem to be rid of rather than potential to be realized. It is important to see our youth as God sees them and not how society sees them. King David was seen by his father, his brothers, his king, and the assembly of God's people as a youth with little to offer. When youth are seen that way, who would be willing to waste time working with them? God shows no partiality. He does not choose who to use based on their age but on their availability. Valuing young people is about finding youth who are present, available, and hungry to learn and help. Investing in our youth and teaching them how to read and understand the Bible is powerful for the entire church.

The Bible is filled with examples of young people making impactful inputs into the work of the Lord. If Daniel and his three young friends were able to serve in the royal courts of Israel and Babylon, surely there are young people able to serve in leadership roles in our congregations. If young Jeremiah can be called to the prophetic ministry as a youth, then surely there are youth whom God can send out to preach and teach his Word today. If Samuel was called to the priesthood as a young man, then young people can be called to serve as worship leaders and ministers in our churches today. Even as a part of preparation for their bar/bat mitzvah, many Jewish youth memorize the Torah (the first five books of the Bible). This ought to change our view of what youth are capable of if only we are willing to put the time in with them.[2]

Many of the challenges faced by youth in urban centers can be addressed by recognizing the principle over the particulars. The young person who is always ready to fight, the one constantly talking, the one who does anything to garner attention are all showing youth workers their particular issues. But what if we focused not on the particular issues but identified the principle behind their actions? For instance, the principle behind the fighter may reveal them as a defender or a protector in principle rather than the problem of a combatant.

The teen who constantly has to talk in principle may just be a communicator rather than an interrupter. It may be helpful for this person who likes to talk to be given opportunities to speak during the programs for the ministry. For youth who seem to need attention or want to be the center of focus, the principle behind it can be one who wants to participate rather than spectate. Praying for God to change the way we see the youth we serve may yield helpful revelations. Gaining the support of the entire church around the youth ministry sometimes requires a willingness to exalt their capabilities and defend their honor.

DEFEND NOT DESPISE

Youth are unique, and we must recognize they are developing into adulthood with the need of our assistance. Because many of us as adults are disconnected from the season of our youth, it is sometimes more difficult for us to identify with what young people are struggling with today. As a result, sometimes we can unknowingly minimize their value when we would do better defending them. The generation gap is apparent among many congregations. Adult worshipers ask, "Why do they play their music so loud? Why do they wear their pants hanging down? Why is this hip-hop music so degrading and vulgar? Why is their language so perverse? Why are they always fighting? Why are they behaving like that on social media?" Instead of degrading young people, often forgetting we were the same way as teenagers, we would do better to learn how to protect, preserve, and prove to young people who they really are and what they can do for God based on how they are personally wired.

Creating a culture of respect for the young Christians we serve would go a long way in developing their acceptance of our ministry to them. Youth leaders are in a unique space to create a culture of reverence for the young people. Many things can be done to ensure this, but the idea is to keep the youth before the eyes of the congregation. When we talk about our youth often and frequently reveal to the church what they are doing, it helps everyone to have the youth and their needs on their minds. It will be difficult to forget about the youth if youth workers keep them before the eyes of the congregation.

Anything that can be done to keep the youth before the eyes of the congregation will help to create a culture in the church that will value and respect them more.

This is especially important if the youth are worshiping separately from the adult congregation. Hanging up pictures of youth events and activities or posting on social media are ways of letting the entire church see what God is doing through the youth. Anything that can be done to keep the youth before the eyes of the congregation will help to create a culture in the church that will value and respect them more. Those who are not seen are often not valued. Those who are disconnected will often be displaced and isolated. I am glad that when I was a youth in ministry there were many in our church who advocated for the teenagers, spoke up for us, and defended us rather than despised us. When both youth and adults in the congregation defend the need for vibrant youth ministry, it is easier for others to invest in whatever ways they can as well.

WORTH THE INVESTMENT

Like any good soldier, it takes time, training, resources, and consistency to raise strong young disciples. In God's covenant with the world, he promised never to destroy the earth through a flood again. God declared that "as long as the earth endures, seedtime and harvest, cold and heat, summer and winter, day and night will never cease" (Genesis 8:22). The principle here is that there are seasons needed to nurture the world in order to enable it for habitation. Spring is usually the seed-sowing time. Summer brings forth an increase of light throughout the days and heat provides nurturance to create a climate for the development of fruit in the earth. Fall will bring harvest, resources, and nutrition for the perseverance of those inhabiting the earth, and winter will bring an end to crop bearing and allow the earth to rest. The design of the world helps us to see that if we invest time in sowing seeds and watering and nurturing crops, then we will eventually produce a harvest to keep us going. This is also true spiritually as we sow into the lives of others, in this particular case, the youth.

The law of sowing and reaping is seedtime and harvest, which means between seed and harvest there is this thing we call "time." Developing young soldiers for God does not occur accidentally. It happens intentionally by those willing to sow into them. Along with sowing, there will be time between our labor until we begin seeing the developing of fruit in the lives of our youth. The problem for many of us is that sometimes workers give up and quit before the fruit in the lives of their youth is visible.

The turnover rate of youth workers is high in many urban churches, and as a result, many of these churches stop or cancel their youth ministries altogether. You do not have to have a youth church service at your church to raise young disciples, but if you do not have a youth church service, the adult church should be careful to regularly preach to and address issues that are relevant to youth as well. Because a lot of youth workers are involved in youth ministry for fraudulent reasons, the commitment to the youth dwindles.

On the other hand, there are many in the congregation of our churches who are perfect for serving the youth and do not even know it. You may feel like you don't have enough in common with youth to serve them, but you have a heart for youth and want to see them grow in God's grace. Finding commonality with youth is not always a prerequisite for serving them. Some may feel like the youth ministry at your church is not thriving and the work would be too hard, so it is easier to find other ways to serve the congregation. Then there are also believers in the church who feel like they are too old to serve young people.

But what if what the youth need is not your youth because they have their own? What if what they really needed was your wisdom and experience that comes with age because that it is what they lack? Youth are well worth our investments in their lives. Many churches need people in their congregations to find a way to support their youth and the youth ministries. With time, funding, teaching, counseling, and training, both youth and workers will all support God's aim to raise young disciples and strengthen your church. There are ways you can discern whether youth ministry is right for you.

DISCERNING HOW TO SERVE

If you have been convinced that youth are worth the investment of your time and labor and that their potential is to be valued not despised, then a good next step for you is to pray for guidance on how you could participate or perhaps serve in God's work among the youth. Just like parenthood, youth ministry requires committed, continual care, and cultivation. The call to serve the youth ought to be a thoughtful commitment because youth need consistent leaders to help them grow. Our church designs youth ministries for high school students, although some youth ministries include junior high students.

For purposes of understanding this work, the youth ministries that I have participated in and of which I speak of in this book consist of teenagers only (ages thirteen to nineteen) or typically eighth grade through the end of high school. This means that every year a portion of the youth will move on to college or the adult ministry of the congregation. Every year new youth will become a part of the youth ministry. It also means that every four or five years you go through a high school cycle and cultural changes. This often requires at least a five-year commitment from the youth workers and youth pastor to be in tune with the culture of the church and their youth. After the five-year mark is usually when the work of the ministry with the youth will become more impactful. The problem is many quit well before year five and fail to see the fruit of their labor. Once a youth pastor leaves, the culture is rebuilt by the next leader and it starts all over again.

The role of a youth worker is important because like an infant needs the mother to cultivate them from infancy to the next stage, youth need workers to cultivate them from high school to adulthood. Usually, the most effective workers in the spiritual transformation of youth have been those who have served in their role for at least five years. This is why a discernment of calling is important. Some serve youth ministries because they were asked to serve. However, our commitment to doing youth ministry ought to require more than merely meeting a volunteer need. Some members of the church serve in youth ministry because they are being paid, but serving the youth should also be about more than a job. In urban areas where youth are increasingly experiencing absent fathers and parents who are on drugs, incarcerated, or incapable of being present in their lives, they need a consistent presence from those caring for their souls in the church. It takes time to build trusting relationships with young people and, therefore, commitment to serve long-term is essential to making a great impact in the lives of individual youth.

Authentic ministry flows from the heart, so if a person doesn't have the gift, calling, and/or passion for young people, it is probably best not to be a hands-on youth ministry worker. This does not mean that they would be unable to serve their young people in other indirect ways. Youth can be indirectly served by the giving of resources to the needs of young people or by helping to advocate for young people in the church. Others can assist with the administrative work that benefits the youth ministry, among many other needs that can be addressed to help the youth ministry but if young people are going to grow in discipleship, they need people who are gifted, passionate, and called to work directly with them.

At our church, we use three factors to help place members in key areas of service to the congregation: gifts, calling, and passion. We look for at least two of the three to be in alignment with the ministries where people serve. Calling is determined by the internal desire of the believer and the external affirmation of that call. In other words, if a person senses internally a calling to serve in our youth ministry, that alone would not be sufficient to place them there. The next question will be whether others in the church recognize the gifts necessary for that ministry in them. Sometimes there are and sometimes there are not, but there is safety in a multitude of counselors to discern with them. Usually, other members of the congregation can sense calling and gifting in members who belong to the church. However, regardless of whether there is both internal and external confirmation of a person's sense of call, we also want their sense of calling to be matched with their giftedness or passion for the call or both.

Giftedness is exposed by what the church has witnessed in a member's contributions. However, a person can have a gift but not have a passion for what they are gifted to do. Just because a person is gifted at something does not mean they have a passion for doing it in the church. For instance, a person who is a high school teacher may be gifted working with teenagers but though this person may work with youth daily as an occupation, it doesn't mean they have a desire to leave work and come serve youth in their church. Passion should always be one of the factors. No one should serve an area of the church that they are not passionate about.

A person who has a strong sense of a calling, sufficient gifts that are useful for youth ministry, and a resilient passion to serve teenagers, would be recommended to go ahead and commit to work with youth for the long haul. Calling is important, but so are passion and giftedness in discerning a calling to youth ministry. Usually, the affirmation of at least two out of the three factors will be sufficient for discerning whether you should serve in the youth ministry. Youth must not be despised, forgotten about, or counted out. They must be served, committed to, and raised into maturity for God. But as one discerns whether to serve and prepare to begin serving the youth, it is important to make sure that they are clear on what youth ministry is and what serving the youth is all about.

A DEEPER DIVE

The following questions are intended for reflection in order to help reverse the trend of despising or underestimating the potential of teenagers in the church.

1. In what ways can you promote the potential of youth in ministry at your church?
2. How do the adults in your church demonstrate that they value youth and youth ministry?

3. Can you identify ministry opportunities in your congregation that youth are uniquely gifted and designed to address?

4. What are the strengths of young people in your ministry that you can share and promote throughout the church?

4

DEFINING
YOUTH MINISTRY

---

*"Just as the Son of Man did not come
to be served, but to serve, and to give
his life as a ransom for many."*

MATTHEW 20:28

IN MY EARLY YEARS AS A TEENAGE BELIEVER, God used
me in a variety of ways in the city of Chicago and areas around
the country. I was unaware of the privilege of being a part of a
vibrant youth ministry. In the youth ministry at the Salem
Baptist Church of Chicago, I was given opportunities to lead as
a teenager. Our youth were highly valued and extremely utilized
in our youth church services as well as the corporate worship
with the adult congregation. As a result of the fruit of discipleship, I was given frequent opportunities to speak in public
settings and to teach even adults as a teenager. I was also ap-
pointed a deacon in the congregation alongside the church

leaders during adult worship services on Sundays and Wednesday evening Bible classes.

I would often receive invitations to share my testimony of how I came to faith in Jesus or to talk to people about the gospel (both adults and youth). One time, I remember being invited to speak at a particular church on the west side of Chicago. When I arrived, the disinterest of the youth was very apparent. There were about twelve children, four teenagers, and seventeen adults ranging in age from fifty to seventy. The program began with a deacon's devotion. He hummed, groaned, and moaned the entire time with his words being difficult to understand. Some of the teens were smirking and holding back their laughs while others were cold asleep. The children were running around the sanctuary playing and paying no attention. Even some of the adults were eating, drinking coffee, and walking in and out of the room as if they were preoccupied with something else.

A child came to give the prayer and stood there silent for what seemed like an eternity while the adults tried to get them to talk. Finally, a teenager was asked to pray, and he did not do much better. He clearly didn't want to be there, he seemed embarrassed in front of his peers, and he mumbled a few words under his breath while his two friends were laughing at him. A woman came up to speak and began to yell and holler at the young people about getting right with God or going to hell. Then a man probably in his forties came up and performed the most horrific rap in the history of hip-hop—a Jesus rap with a drum beat and a 1974 Kurtis Blow style that made me cringe for it to be over.

This was what this church called youth ministry. I don't share this story to belittle this congregation or make light of what they do, because at least they were trying to do something for their youth. The issue, however, is that many people trying to work with youth do not have a philosophy to lead what they are doing and are in need of resources to help them improve their work. I appreciate the effort of a church trying to do something for their youth, but the problem is they had no idea what they were doing. This event clearly had no youthful input or biblical guidance, and they apparently perceived it as youth ministry simply because they had some kids there.

Defining youth ministry is foundational to accomplishing the aim of youth ministry. This chapter provides a practical working definition for doing youth ministry that will increase the value of youth ministry among both youth and youth workers in the church. I was raised in a youth ministry where we defined it not as ministry to youth but as youth doing ministry. When we see youth ministry in this way, it helps to increase the value of youth ministry and guide what we focus on doing in youth ministry. Youth ministry ought to be youth doing ministry. Youth doing ministry is productive, powerful, and what we ought to aim for in our ministry work with youth.

CONTEMPORARY YOUTH MINISTRY

Youth ministry is a contemporary term used to describe a particular ministry of the church by which the spiritual needs of younger members, usually teenagers ages thirteen to nineteen, are addressed. The phrase *youth ministry* is not mentioned in the Bible, but neither are adult ministry, women's ministry, marriage ministry, or most other auxiliary focuses of ministry we engage in our congregations. Although churches practice youth ministry in a variety of ways, the idea of youth ministry is in fact a biblical concept.

The Bible gives us instructions for teaching the younger generations, instructing them in God's commands and leading the youth in their walk of faith. The church is tasked with sharing the responsibility of ministering to the children and youth along with everyone else. While I define youth ministry as youth doing ministry, I want to be clear that ministering to youth is also important. The biblical concept of ministering to the youth must be the foundation for how we practice youth ministry. This is the reason why a working definition for youth ministry is important for maintaining faithful youth ministry in the church. If we fail to clearly define what youth ministry is in our churches, it can lead to disunity among our teams and unfaithfulness to our God-given assignments. But most importantly, if we do not define what we are doing, then it becomes impossible to measure our success.

There is a proverb in Amos 3:3 that teaches us that two cannot walk together unless they agree. In order for a church to do youth ministry together they must agree on what youth ministry is. Defining youth ministry will bring unity to our teams because we can agree about what the work is. However, if we do not define youth ministry how can we be in agreement or determine our faithfulness to youth ministry. One person's understanding of youth ministry can and will be different from another's idea of youth ministry.

If we do not clearly define what our church's aim is in youth ministry, it will be merely impossible to reach a goal. No team can accomplish an assignment that has not been given. Youth ministries can benefit from the words of Habakkuk 2:2 to write the vision and make it plain so that others can run with it and fulfill their calling. Faithfulness to the ministry can be fulfilled only when the assignment is clear. I want to explore some of the trends in the development of contemporary youth ministry in the United States to help take a deeper dive into our working definition for youth ministry.

THE PRACTICE OF YOUTH MINISTRY

Contemporary youth ministry grew out of parachurch organizations that were being developed to reach youth in society and raise them up as disciples in the church. Perhaps the best known of these organizations was the Young Men's Christian Association (YMCA), which originally began in London in 1844.[1] Becoming a global ministry, the YMCA, and later YWCA (Young Women's Christian Association), gained traction in the United States among other ministries for youth.

However, the best and majority work was among the White youth: "As their organizational structure suggests, the YMCA and YWCA movements were initially committed to a rigid separation of the genders. The same was true of ethnicity. African American young people were segregated by the Ys into separate but not equal facilities until the 1940s, and much longer in some settings."[2]

As it was for the origin of Black churches, Black youth ministries had to be developed by Black people to look out for the interests of their own youth.

The success of organizations like Youth for Christ and Young Life in the 1940s and 1950s led to local churches developing ministries in their own congregations to help youth become faithful followers of Christ.[3] What does it mean and what does it look like for youth to be faithful followers of Christ? At minimum, it looks like youth living for God and serving God through his church. Now that youth ministry in local congregations is a cultural norm, we see that many congregations are developing what they are calling youth ministry, but what are these so called youth ministries in our churches doing?

For some churches the practice of youth ministry is Sunday school or discipleship classes offered to youth. Other churches do youth services usually on the fifth Sundays of the month in collaboration with the adult congregation. Often these services are developed by adults and the youth are told what to do in the service. There is little ownership by the youth and one service every three or four months is just not enough. Often when speakers are brought in to preach to the youth, they typically preach to the adults about adult issues while ignoring the teenagers and the youth are left bored, disinterested, and left out of what the congregation is calling a youth ministry.

Some churches devote an annual budget to their teenagers and give them separate space for their own worship gatherings, often with a youth director, minister, or youth pastor on staff. In these situations, there is usually a calendar of events for the youth and teaching is regularly designed for them, but does this mean youth ministry is happening? The answer will depend upon how youth ministry is defined. If youth ministry is defined as anything the church does for those who are adolescents at the church, then sure, everything I mentioned above is authentic youth ministry. However, is this what God has in mind for what youth ministry or any ministry should be accomplishing in the church?

As adults it is important that we are intentional not to highjack the worship experience that should be designed for our youth. We as adults can often get youth event speakers based on what appeals to us and not the youth. We can plan and implement each youth event and activity without any input from the teenagers at all. Other times youth are invited to share their suggestions, but their ideas and desires are not valued or given any place in the actual implementation of the events. I believe these disappointments happen because we define youth ministry as ministry to youth. This is not a good definition. When we approach youth ministry like adults trying to minister to teenagers, it is easier to despise and undervalue what the youth have to offer. I would like to expound on my practical definition for youth ministry to increase the value and potential of the youth in our churches.

DEFINITION FOR THE PRACTICE OF YOUTH MINISTRY

The definition of youth ministry is not the same as the mission of a youth ministry. A mission statement is designed to address what a youth ministry does, not what youth ministry is. Likewise, a definition for a youth ministry is not the same as a vision for youth ministry. While the mission is what the youth ministry does, the vision is what the youth ministry wants to accomplish by what it does. The mission are the seeds sown and the vision is the fruit of the seed we sow. A definition for youth ministry identifies what youth ministry is at its core. Mission is what the youth ministry does, vision is what the youth ministry fulfills, but youth ministry itself is how we identify it all. If we are going to practice youth ministry, it should be properly defined, and I have found in my years of youth ministry experience that defining youth ministry as youth doing ministry portrays this work in a way that increases the value of the young people's actual and potential contributions in the church. Youth ministry is exactly that—youth in ministry. Spiritually mature youth love God, live for God, and serve God in ministry. When our youth mature, they will inevitably carry out ministry in our congregations and contribute to the work of the entire church.

Youth doing ministry is what youth ministry is all about. When youth ministry is designed this way, it changes everything.

When adults who practice youth ministry define it as "ministering to youth," it gives value to what the adults do to help youth. However, when youth ministry is defined as "youth doing ministry," the focus and the value shifts to the youth themselves. They are seen as the ones who are "doing." When the youth are seen as the ones who are doing ministry, the youth workers see their role as investing in the youth because their ministry is done through them.

When youth ministry is seen this way, what a church does will not be identified as youth ministry unless the youth are involved in doing the ministry. This helps to raise the value of the youth among the people in our congregations. If youth ministry is about youth doing ministry, then youth can no longer be undervalued, overlooked, or despised in your ministry. When youth ministry is seen as youth doing ministry, then youth have to be trained, discipled, and developed to do the same work as everyone else in the congregation.

Youth workers will no longer see their roles as babysitting or entertaining teenagers but rather discipling and training youth. When youth ministry is defined this way then young people can have ownership in the ministry and involvement in the planning and implementation of the ministry work. This helps young people to understand the importance of their contributions in the church and garner more involvement from them. This not only increases the worth of the youth, but it also intensifies the interests of the youth in what the church is doing. As we recognize youth ministry as youth doing ministry, planning for youth ministry events and activities will be different. The excitement among youth around the events of the church will become different and the participation of youth in the events of the church will increase.

Now that we understand youth ministry as youth doing ministry, then the next thing we must define is what do we mean by *ministry.* Our English term *ministry* is translated from the biblical work *dia-ko-nos*, which means "a servant." The New Testament idea of ministry means to serve God and others in honor of God. In Matthew 20:28, Jesus says to his disciples, "Just as the Son of Man did not come to be served, but to serve, and to give his life as a ransom for many."

When we speak of ministry, Jesus is our ultimate example. If anyone deserves to be served, Jesus, who is God our Creator, deserves to be served, but rather than being served, Jesus the Creator chose to come down to earth and serve his own creation. Service to God is what we call ministry. So, youth doing ministry basically translates to youth who are serving God. There are many ways that youth who are in different places in the journey of their faith can still serve God. Scripture helps to guide us in understanding God's aim for the practice of youth ministry or ministering to and through youth.

THEOLOGY FOR THE PRACTICE OF YOUTH MINISTRY

The challenge of youth ministry for us as adults is that while trying to assist, we can often get in the way of allowing the youth to serve. A central theology for the practice of youth ministry is discipleship. It is all about helping our youth become learners and followers of Christ in the church. The faithful spiritual development of youth allows our congregations to develop youth to do ministry rather than trying to do ministry in order to develop our youth. Chapter seven will go into more depth around the issue of discipleship with youth, but our theology of the practice of youth ministry must factor in spiritual growth. As youth workers we are practicing youth ministry when we are helping the youth to grow spiritually to fulfill their service to God. Youth should be esteemed highly enough to be taught biblical doctrine and spiritual disciplines. When they are despised because of their youth, their discipleship is neglected. God made this need for discipling the young apparent to Israel, the people of God in the Old Testament.

One of the key declarations of the Jewish people in the Old Testament is the Shema of Deuteronomy 6.[4] God instructs his people to pass their faith, his commandments, and teachings down to the younger generations: "Love the LORD your God with all your heart and with all your soul and with all your strength. These commandments that I give you today are to be on your hearts. Impress them on your children. Talk about them when you sit at home and when you walk along the road, when you lie down and when you get up" (Deuteronomy 6:5-7).

The first principle of note from this passage is that youth ministry or the development for youth ministry is to begin in the house through the parents or guardians of the youth. Moses assures the people of God that it is their responsibility to teach God's commands to their children and for parents to discuss them with their children at home daily. This means that youth ministry must involve the parents of the youth. Youth ministries or youth pastors that are not seeking to know the parents or collaborate with the parents are less likely to succeed in the spiritual development of the youth. The church in partnership and relationship with the parents is to unite in the spiritual development of their youth who will be established to serve the Lord in their teens but also as future adult leaders in the church.

Youth workers must be careful not to water down the gospel or underestimate the ability of the young people to receive sound doctrine. We can teach teenagers as if they were adults, allow teenagers to teach as if they were adults, and help develop the theologies of our youth as if they were adults. All of the fun activities, games, and getaways we do for our young people have their place, but as a foundation, youth ministries would do well to develop discipleship opportunities in everything they possibly can.

Growing up in youth ministry, we had a hip-hop group, but Bible study was a part of that ministry. No one could rap in the ministry unless they studied the Scriptures with us or were faithful in church. We had a fraternal step team, but studying the Scriptures was priority and included in their rehearsals. The same is true with our basketball team, the youth choir, and any other auxiliary ministry focus we had. So, while those looking from the outside in saw only the fun and entertainment (rapping, stepping, singing, dancing, etc.), those on the inside knew that everything they did came through the Word of God, and they used their gifts as worship offerings to the Lord.

OAKDALE COVENANT CHURCH YOUTH MINISTRY

During my seminary years, I became a member of the Oakdale Covenant Church in the Auburn Gresham community on the south side of Chicago. After serving in the youth ministry at the Salem Baptist Church for fifteen years and as a youth minister in Gary, Indiana, I landed at Oakdale for some years following. I was in my mid-thirties and had a passion for the church and urban ministry. A year after joining Oakdale, I became an associate minister on their ministerial roster. At this time, I was in school at North Park Theological Seminary on the north side of the city. My plan was to serve a congregation as a lead pastor when I finished my master's in divinity. When it was time to graduate, I had served Oakdale faithfully for those three years. However, I never served at any point in the youth department. I assisted with preaching and teaching during the Wednesday night Bible classes and evangelistic counseling of new members, and I taught Sunday school classes and new members orientation.

When I graduated from seminary, God made it clear that his plans for me were different than my own. On April 1, 2008, I suffered the greatest blow I had faced in life when my father passed away just weeks before I graduated. Things were going well, and I had several options of churches to pastor, but all of the offers were out of town. With the loss of my father and the role that I played in our family, it was not a good season to move out of the city. So, I turned down the offers and prayed for God to help me find a church to serve in Chicago. Little did I know, at this same time the youth pastor on staff at Oakdale was being called to pastor a church and was stepping down from his role. I was approached by the senior pastor, Dr. D. Darrel Griffin, about joining the staff as their youth pastor. I wanted to be a senior pastor and I could have turned it down, but the truth was that I had a lot of youth ministry experience as a youth won off the streets from youth ministry to a youth pastor developing other teenagers in the faith.

I valued youth and youth ministry, so it made sense that this is what God wanted me to do. I accepted the role and would continue in it for the next nine years before organizing the church plant where I serve as senior pastor today, Kingdom Covenant Church Chicago. Today many who are called to serve as youth pastors for some reason see it as less than the role of a senior pastor and either reject the opportunity or accept the role as a temporary job until they can find something else rather than a serious call to shepherd the youth. You cannot fool young people. The youth know when we care about them. The youth know when we are invested in them, and one of the worst things anyone can do is serve as a youth pastor when they do not have a heart to work with young people. I had to lay down my desire to serve as a senior pastor and go back to youth ministry for another nine years.

In my first year at Oakdale alone, the attendance of young men in youth church tripled. By the time I left, we averaged over one hundred youth in weekly worship. The attendance of youth retreats tripled and most importantly youth became serious about God and grew in their relationship with the Lord. We developed a Youth Church Team (YCT), where youth were the leaders and would come up with creative ways to have youth church service and they would plan all of the youth ministry events. We met at six every Saturday morning to plan worship, retreats, and activities for the youth of the church. We met early simply so that I could see their hunger and commitment, and they came regardless of how early we met. The youth church team would appoint a YCT president each year who would take the lead, and the adult workers would empower these youth by listening to their ideas, taking what they said seriously, and helping to implement them.

Youth put together theatrical events based on Scripture but through the culture of youth. They taught the Word of God and led other youth to faith in Christ both in the church and outside of the church in their communities. They put together themed worship services on Sundays that were fun and unique, such as Sports Sundays when they wore the garb of their favorite sports team, Pajama Sundays, or Seventies Sunday, where youth and youth workers dressed in 1970s attire, decorated the youth church space in seventies style, and used the theme to convey biblical ideas and challenge young people's faith. It was creative and all done in fun, but we made sure that the main focus through it all was the Word of God and the transformation of lives. Youth church and events should be fun. This is very important. Sometimes adults can make God and church boring to young people. We want youth to come back because they had so much fun, but we should use the fun as a means to minister the truth. At Oakdale we began to see hardened youth worship and weep in the presence of God without shame or embarrassment. The youth prayed for one another and put together their own fasting schedules and prayer calls, all because they became the means of doing ministry and not the object of adults doing ministry. Youth were able to see how church worked and how to lead and put things together because we helped them become leaders.

I can honestly say that I have seen many of these youth grow and continue to lead the church today as adults because their input was valued when they were teens. Many are continuing to serve Oakdale today as adults. Others are serving in various congregations in the city and other states, but their time being nurtured as youth is what prepared them for what they are doing for God as adults today. One of the youths I served when I was youth pastor at Oakdale became a youth pastor there later on. That is the goal, to mature youth into leaders. Glory to God for how he has raised and equipped young people to serve his kingdom.

The youth we serve in ministry should be viewed as youth being evangelized, equipped, and empowered to do ministry. The idea is to make sure the youth are reading, understanding, and applying the Bible in their lives and serving their church. Youth should no longer be viewed as babies who are totally dependent on us but as potential ministers, lay leaders, theologians, or colaborers and apologists for the church. When youth ministry is seen in this light, youth are esteemed higher and become the foundation for the work that is to be done for the Lord through them.

A DEEPER DIVE

The following communications are intended for reflection in order to help reverse the trend of adults doing ministry for youth instead of youth doing ministry themselves.

1. How does this chapter's definition of youth ministry inform how you are currently doing youth ministry at your church?

2. Can you identify youth who are doing ministry at your church? How can you leverage their work to increase the value of youth ministry in the eyes of the congregation?

3. What are some ways you can support the youth ministering in your church?

4. Who are the youth you can identify as active in the work of the church?

5

BELIEVERS
NOT BABIES

When I was a child, I talked like a child,
I thought like a child, I reasoned like a child.
When I became a man, I put the ways
of childhood behind me.

1 CORINTHIANS 13:11

AFTER ALL OF THE YEARS I SERVED in youth ministry, when I started Kingdom Covenant Church Chicago, I imagined that building a thriving youth ministry would be easy. However, I learned it takes more than experience and knowledge to build a vibrant youth ministry. It takes a committed community of believers with a heart and passion for young people. It takes a group of people to see youth as the next in line to be used by God. Having a commitment from a group of believers to give significant time to serving the youth is critical.

Our congregation, like many others, wanted to see committed ongoing ministry designed to and through youth, but few were willing to commit to that ongoing work themselves. This is becoming more common in church plants and urban and traditional African American churches across the country. Every congregation has people serving adults, and I believe that every congregation should have people serving youth and children. As churches, we can bring attention to the teenagers as well as encourage and inspire the church to visualize the untapped potential in the youth. Youth workers who view their youth as little children will not treat their youth as contributors, and if youth will be treated as contributors, we need to see them as more than babies.

FAITH DEVELOPMENT

In my third year as the youth pastor of Oakdale Covenant Church, we had been having youth church weekly for two years. We brought on a new musician who brought her children to youth church with her. Her youngest child was about ten years old, and although she was young, she had such a heart for God. Although this child was not yet in her preteens, she preached with a sincere heart to the teenagers, and on one particular Sunday under the inspiration of the Holy Spirit, she asked me if she could say something to the church. As her tear-filled eyes were watering her face, she began to speak about the goodness of God and the importance of young people knowing and loving him back. But what was even more powerful than her ministering to our youth was the attention she gained from them. A ten-year-old child captured the attention of sixteen- and seventeen-year-old youth. Some came to the altar to pray and even those who are usually jokesters were yielding to what

God was doing at the moment through a ten-year-old Christian child.

This young girl was close to God, and she contributed to our ministry every week even though the official age for youth ministry at the church was ninth through twelfth grades. This young girl began to be forced to go to the children's church simply because of her age, and she didn't like it. Everyone knew the development of her faith, but because she was seen by the workers as nothing but a baby, they began forcing her into a community that she had spiritually outgrown. I fought to liberate this young lady to attend youth church with us because that is where she was growing and experiencing God regardless of her age. The church eventually realized this and allowed her to attend church with the youth. She contributed greatly to our ministry over the next four years. Today she is a young adult who just graduated from college and continues to faithfully serve the Lord.

Let me pause and say that this example also illustrates the fact that children are being despised. The children's ministry here had a long range of development among children ages two through twelve years old. When grouping these ages into one church experience, it can be hard to balance what is done and how it is done to meet every child where they are in one service. If the children's church would have been able to see the development of this young lady and other children who were developing faster than others, it could have been a great opportunity to adjust some things in children's ministry where they could be more comfortable there.

When we can only see youth as babes, it becomes difficult to realize their capabilities for the kingdom. What I mean is that seeing youth as babies implies that they need more from us than they actually do. They are not fully developed adults, but they are not little babies either. It is worth repeating that this is not about devaluing children because they can contribute to the church as well in their own ways, but we must also acknowledge that the season of adolescent years is further along and youth can be given more responsibility in the church. Youth workers should demand more in ministry than what is typically capable of a six year old, eight year old, or even many eleven year olds.

Seeing youth as babies also hinders our focus on training them, which causes us to nurse them to give their parents a break instead of nurturing their faith for kingdom impact. When our youth can be seen as mature Christians instead of little children, their value is restored, our investments can bear fruit, and their transformation is inevitable. The same is true of children, just on a different level. God can and does use young people, often to cultivate the faith of their parents, teachers, peers, and even their youth group leaders. They may be youthful, but that does not mean they are not useful.

YOUNG BUT USEFUL

In 1 Corinthians 13:11, Paul declared, "When I was a child, I talked like a child, I thought like a child, I reasoned like a child. When I became a man, I put the ways of childhood behind me." Notice Paul did not say, "When I became eighteen years old, I put childhood behind me." He said, "When I became a man," or another way to say it is, "When I matured, I put away childish things." It is not age but maturity that reveals our growth. Paul is making the point that his speech, thinking, and rationalization developed over the years to the point where he no longer acted like he did as a child. This is also true of teenagers. They are still developing into adulthood, but they have developed from childhood into their season of adolescence. They are no longer babies. They are less dependent than children and can be entrusted with more and can do more than young children. Youth are young, but they are also useful.

At first glance, this passage from Paul can seem like a deviation from his discourse on spiritual gifts. Both in the previous chapter and the following chapter, Paul is discussing the issue of spiritual gifts. In chapter twelve, the focus on spiritual gifts is about the diversity of gifts that each member of the church has and how they should function in a unified way for the edification of the church as a whole. In chapter fourteen, the issue of spiritual gifts is about how they should function in an orderly manner for the development of the church.

Chapter thirteen opens with a focus on the display of love, but it is not a deviation from the spiritual gifts. Rather it is a demonstration on how the gifts should operate through love. The force of this chapter is not only gift development but character development. Paul opens in verse one by saying, "If I speak in the tongues of men or of angels, but do not have love, I am only a resounding gong or a clanging cymbal." In verses four through eight, Paul provides a description of love as a mark of spiritual maturity, stating in verse seven that love "always protects, always trusts, always hopes, always perseveres."

Paul begins to transition to the end of this focus by saying, "Love never fails. But where there are prophecies, they will cease; where there are tongues, they will be stilled; where there is knowledge, it will pass away. For we know in part and we prophesy in part, but when completeness comes, what is in part disappears" (1 Corinthians 13:8-10).
Paul seems to be comparing the ceasing of spiritual gifts with the ever existence of love and thus the superiority of developing

our love. This is when he makes the statement of verse eleven that "when I became a man, I put the ways of childhood behind me." Like Paul we are all developing. Developing in our thoughts, in our rationale, and developing in our gifts, our love, and our ways. For a parent, their child will always be their child regardless of age, but the parenting methods will have to adjust as the child develops and matures. It is, therefore, helpful to recognize the development of the adolescents we serve and guide them based upon their capacity in that season.

No youth are useless, but many youths are undervalued.

When we see the potential of God in every one of our youths regardless of their trials and traumas, their value begins to surge in our eyes, and we can easily commit to investing our lives into theirs. No youth are useless, but many youths are undervalued. The consequence of undervalued or despised youth is they will always be underutilized. Paul charged his young pupil, Timothy, not to allow anyone to despise his youth or undervalue him because he was young. The way for our youth to demand and garner respect according to 1 Timothy 4:12 is by being an example of a believer. This is what youth workers are there to nurture. We have to invest in the spiritual growth of our teenagers until they are living out their faith because when they are living out their faith, they become examples for the believers.

SETTING EXAMPLES IN THE CHURCH

Youth and advocates for youth have a role to play in helping congregations respect the spiritual potential of younger Christians. Paul lists five ways to advocate as a model for our youth ministries today.

Speech. Paul charged Timothy not to allow anyone to despise him because he was younger. To be successful in this endeavor, Paul suggests that Timothy would have to set the believers an example of the Christian life. The first way young people are to set an example for the church is in their speech. If you want to know where your young people are, all you have to do is listen to their speech. You will see in their conversations if they are close to God or if they are closer to the world. One way to help youth be examples in their speech is to provide as many opportunities as you can to allow them to speak as they are growing. Allowing youth to share their testimonies, encouraging stories, Scriptures, exhortations, teaching, or anything that can encourage and edify others is very powerful and strengthens the church.

Behavior. Paul exhorts Timothy to be an example in his actions as well. The next way young people can set an example for the church is in their conduct or behavior. The behavior of youth who know and love God will be distinct from the behavior of youth who do not. The real example of the believer is a changed life. There are youth leaders who may never say it out loud, but they do not believe that their youth will ever change. The truth is the gospel changes people, and the gospel can change anyone. To not believe this is to despise your youth.

Due to common conditions that exist in many low-income communities of color, youth are more easily exposed to the prevalent problems of their environment. Youth violence is perpetuating traumatrigenic communities. The change of behavior begins with the changing of minds, and youth workers can affect the change of young people's minds if they are willing to put in the time. One helpful way is to have transparency with the youth. Many youth workers are perceived as if they never did anything wrong or never have any struggles. But it is a powerful thing to be willing to share our life stories of transformation and struggle, if not with a group then with individual teens.

All it takes to revolutionize a youth ministry is to have one seriously sold-out-for-God young person. A youth ministry will thrive when young people live the Christian life openly. When I came off the streets, I was blessed to witness two of my childhood friends who later became rival gang enemies come to faith in Christ as well. My homie who went by the name of Bo and another homie I will not mention by name came to faith at the same time. We collaborated to reach a world that was typically beyond the grasp of most church people. Our conduct was just different.

We were not afraid of gunfire because we had been in gun-fights. We were not afraid to go into dangerous areas because we felt more at home in these spaces. We knew the killers in the neighborhood personally. We were the dope dealers, the gang-sters, those who robbed people, and now we were young Christians with no fear of death or harm. We didn't live in fear when we were lost, and with God on our side, we were willing to do whatever it took to reach those in the darkest places in the world. We launched a grassroots movement of evangelism in our neighborhood.

We would do things like go to a gang meeting and talk about Jesus. We took our youth pastor to a gangster party where he witnessed firsthand teenagers with machine guns, pistols, al-cohol, and drugs. Without fear, Pastor Carey preached the gospel at the party and led young men and women to God. This is not typical Christian behavior or culture. This is not the typical way ministry is being done by the church. But this helped other youth in the ministry to become fearless, to not be ashamed of their faith, and to publicly proclaim Jesus.

We can amplify the godly behavior of our youth by publicly celebrating them. Youth ministries can model behavior by spending time with youth outside of the church setting. I had ample opportunities to learn how to share my faith sitting in restaurants with my pastor who would demonstrate for me how to do it and then give me an opportunity to do it myself. Our behavior as young Christians was authentic even though it was not typical, and the testimonies of lives changed and youth being brought out of the darkest places was something that the adults were not even experiencing in their ministries at the church. This raised the value of youth and their work in the eyes of the church members.

Love. The next way young people can set an example for the church is by their love. Paul encouraged Timothy to be an example of a true Christian by the way he loved others. It is not a stretch to say that what our churches want to see are young people who love God and others. But young people can learn to love God and others based on the way those who work with the young people are loving them. Love is more powerful than most people realize. Love is not only felt—it is seen in our actions.

As youth workers, it is extremely important to love our youth. As a youth pastor, it is even more important to love the youth. It is difficult to effectively challenge, discipline, or try to correct a young person we have not loved immensely first. It is difficult for young people to receive discipline from us when we have not loved them well. As youth workers, when we show love to the youth we serve, they are more likely to display love to others because of the way that they have been loved by us. The love of our youth and the youth's love for others can elevate the church's respect for the youth and youth ministry.

Faith. Paul also exhorted Timothy not to let anyone despise his youthfulness, but to be an example in his faith. I want to spend a bit more time on this example and share a powerful story about the faith of young people. Faith as I define it is the supernatural ability to believe what God says in his Word more than what we see with our eyes. As the church works with teenagers, we have but a short season of their lives to help build their faith. The more often younger people hear the testimony of God and the truth of his Word, the stronger their faith in God can become.

So the story of faith I want to share is about my experience one particular summer, after being a member of the youth ministry at Salem Baptist Church of Chicago for a few years. I was a young leader in the church. It came to my attention that an adult strip club was not only advertising at local high schools, but also it was allowing under-aged youth into their club without IDs. I brought this information to Pastor Carey along with a flyer that was handed out to one of our youths at their high school. We could not believe it. Pastor Carey said we would go there that Friday night to check it out. We prayed and fasted all that week. The plan was to go inside the club with all males to see what was happening and to take a couple of our youth to see if they could get in without an ID. I know this is unorthodox, but it's what we did.

We had a prayer group led by one of our youth leaders whom God called to be a prayer warrior. His name is C. Terrell Wheat, and today he is a pastor and founder of the It Happened in Prayer ministry. He is nationally known for calling God's people back to prayer, and it all started when he was a teenager in the thriving youth ministry of the Salem Baptist Church of Chicago. Terrell, along with about eight other teenagers, prayed outside while I, Pastor Carey, about six other youth workers, and a couple of teenagers went into the club.

Terrell and his group literally laid prostrate on the concrete in front of the club while people going into the club had to step over praying teenagers to go inside the building. Eventually, the staff made them move, but they went on the side of the property and laid their hands on the building and began to pray against the principalities and powers of darkness at work in that place. While they were praying on the outside of the building, our group was observing the action inside. Sure enough, the teenagers we brought with us, even though they looked young and did not have IDs, were allowed into the club. We were protective of them and their eyes, as we were our own, but we needed to be sure that this business was luring underage youth into their adult establishment.

When we came inside the club, there were male strippers on stage. We already made a pact not to expose our eyes to female strippers. It was about 9:30 p.m. at the time. The music was so loud we could not hear each other speak. People in the club were trying to dance with us. They were smoking, drinking, and lusting everywhere. Once we saw evidence that they were knowingly luring teenagers into their establishment, Pastor Carey decided to make a phone call to Rev. Dr. James T. Meeks, the senior pastor of Salem Baptist Church of Chicago. We had been in the club for about fifteen minutes, and the plan from that point was to get the entire church involved, along with the press and community activists to expose this club by drawing attention to their evil. After talking to Pastor Meeks, we were about to leave, but before we left, we all decided to go to the middle of the dance floor where everyone in the club could see, then we made a huge circle, held hands, and began to pray as loud and animated as we could.

We prayed so loud that we could even be heard over the music. During this prayer, it was as if everyone in the club stopped what they were doing to watch and listen to us. We prayed with everything we had. We prayed to cast down strongholds, to expose and expel the enemy. We prayed against lust and perversion. We went into deep spiritual warfare. We must have been praying for about six minutes when we came to the end of the prayer and Pastor Carey closed it out with the words "in Jesus' name, amen," and then everyone said simultaneously, "Amen!"

The lights immediately came on, the music in the club stopped, and we were on our way out, so under the influence of the Holy Spirit we did not realize what was happening. A voice came over the PA system and said, "Sorry about the inconvenience, but we have to close early tonight." When we noticed all of the people walking out behind us to leave the building, we didn't realize that it was because they closed the club. It was only about 10:15 p.m. and the real money makers, the female strippers, had not come out yet. It dawned on us that God had closed the club because of our prayer. Not only did the club close that night, but it closed its business and remains closed to this day. The young people set an example with their faith that God can do anything. We prayed for God to stop and close the club, and that is exactly what he did. This set a fire in our church and inspired the adults as well.

The faith of young people in the power of God brought about this miracle, and it brought about a reverence for youth and an understanding of their potential at our church. God was using young people, and the church came alongside to advocate, fund, and support the work of the youth at the Salem Baptist Church of Chicago. As youth, we believed God. We believed God could do anything, and as we practiced our faith, it made room for miracles like this.

If we want our youth to be examples in their faith, we should do as much as we can to get them to practice their faith publicly. Going on prayer walks in the community can help with this. Having Bible study or preaching that is followed up with actions the church can do is another way. For example, preaching a message about sharing our faith that is followed by an activity in the community that allows youth to share their faith with people or even have public Bible studies outside of the walls of the church. When the youth can see the power of public faith, it increases their passion about their faith, so I encourage youth workers to find ways to make living the faith popular, celebrated, and encouraged among their youth.

Purity. Finally, we learn from Paul's charge to Timothy that one last way for youth to set an example for the church is through their purity. Purity honors God, and as young people choose to honor God by living pure lives, God can use their life to impact others. Also, when young people choose to live a pure life in the sight of God, it is beneficial for the entire congregation. Particularly in the urban context, youth are not known for their purity. Of course, this is the same in many other contexts as well. In many cases, urban youth seem out of control and hedonistic, but when they know God and live pure, it becomes evident that God is real and their lives have been changed. During youth church as well as outreach and evangelism events in schools, prisons, juvenile facilities, and housing projects, among other public settings, I saw youth proudly testify about their abstinence before their peers; they were proud to wait on the spouse God would bless them with or to simply be honoring to God whether they got married or not. For many of them, like myself as a youth, marriage was not even desired at the time. We just wanted to be pure because we loved God and wanted to honor him. I chose to live a pure life because I loved God and wanted to live for him.

Youth were not ashamed to say they were virgins and would not allow other youth to shame them for it. The youth at Salem Baptist Church promoted purity, spoke against pornography, and lived counter to the mainstream youth culture, and this perhaps more than anything raised the value of the youth. The purity of youth can and does help to bring purity to the lives of adults in our churches and even their parents at home. A youth worker struggling with their purity who sees youth fighting to live pure is often convicted that they have to change as well.

Purity is very important in the lives of believers, and as youth workers we should model purity, encourage purity, preach and teach about purity, and allow youth to share testimonies and stories of struggles about purity. In whatever opportunities available, we have to highlight the importance of purity and celebrate and share about the pursuit of purity in the lives of the young people. Our job as youth leaders is not to merely minister to youth but to help youth become active in ministry. Understanding the worth of youth is a necessity for helping churches not to undervalue their youth, but along with the necessity of knowing their worth, we must also understand the necessity of sharing God's Word.

A DEEPER DIVE

The following communications are intended for reflection in order to help reverse the trend of seeing teenagers as too young for congregational ministry.

1. Think of some ways to lead your youth that will give them ownership in the ministry.

2. Can you identify ways that teenagers are being underutilized or held back from their potential at your church or in your ministry?

3. Can you identify ways youth have been held back because they are considered too young in age?

4. Can you identify more practical ways to help your youth be examples for the believer according to the five examples Paul provides for Timothy (1 Timothy 4:12)?

PART TWO

THE NECESSITY OF WORD

6

SOUL FISHING

Jesus called out to them,
"Come, follow me, and I will show you
how to fish for people!"

MATTHEW 4:19 NLT

I BECAME A CHRISTIAN AS A TEENAGER, not because I went to church, but because the church was willing to come to me. Soul winning, or what I like to call *soul fishing*, was a regular practice of the church I attended. I did not come to faith in Jesus overnight. It took some years, but eventually, the gospel saved my soul and God used the youth ministry of the Salem Baptist Church of Chicago to transform my life.

Soul fishing, evangelism, witnessing, and soul winning are all synonymous terms for reaching and drawing people to faith in Christ. While discipleship is about using the gospel to mature believers in their existing faith, soul fishing is about using the gospel to reach those with no faith and helping them to place faith in God. As a young Christian, no one had to tell me I should be sharing my faith with others. I did that automatically. In every conversation I had with people, Jesus was always brought into the discussion. Everywhere I went I talked to people about Jesus and the difference he had made in my life. I was not ashamed, embarrassed, or afraid. I was young and in love with God.

Why would I be afraid when I lived in a war zone and put my life on the line every single day representing my gang and neighborhood affiliation? If I was willing to die on the streets when I was lost, why would I be afraid to live for Jesus on these streets now that I was a Christian? God used my evangelism to help clean up our neighborhood because people stopped hanging out to avoid my coming around preaching to them. I would come outside and see about thirty people on the block, but by the time I got to the corner, no one was there. But there were those I called the "Nick at Night" seekers. They were like Nicodemus in the Bible who came at night to inquire about the gospel. These people often secretly sought me for godly direction. Others would seek me to pray about their court cases or to help with their drug addictions. People were coming to faith in Christ, and many young people in the neighborhood began going to youth church at Salem because of our witness in the neighborhood. Soul fishing is crucial in the building and sustaining of an urban youth ministry.

If the church is unwilling to go and share the good news where the lost youth are, then how do we expect those youth in the community to come to the church or faith in Jesus. Church is not church because of the building. The people of God are the church. Witnessing and sharing the good news at the local park district and on the corners and the blocks in the neighborhood is just as much church as it would be if we were all in the church building together on a Sunday morning. We have to be willing to live, move, exist, and serve in the communities first. If we want to reach youth, we should reach them on their grounds before inviting them to ours.

The lives of youth will not submit to the lordship of Christ without our labor to share God's Word with them. Jesus trained his disciples to fish for souls first by calling them individually to follow him. As youth workers, we should not be calling our youth to do things that we are not committed to doing ourselves. Coaching youth workers to evangelize is just as important as training youth to evangelize. Soul fishing requires the preparation of leaders to reach the lost before we can become leaders to train youth to reach the lost. It is a good thing for youth workers to model how to walk with God and lead others to faith in Jesus. They are not too young to be witnesses.

In the same way Jesus challenged his disciples to become fishers of people, many of the youth of Salem engaged their neighborhoods and practiced soul fishing. The growth of the Salem Baptist Church Youth Ministry was organic and spiritual because, rather than growth through membership exchanges from other churches, the youth ministry developed through youth who had never attended a church before. There are always more youth who are not in church than there are youth who attend churches. There are more than enough fish in the sea to grow a youth ministry. In order to develop and sustain a vibrant youth ministry, there must be dedication to the work of evangelism and outreach among the youth population.

In order to develop and sustain a vibrant youth ministry, there must be dedication to the work of evangelism and outreach among the youth population.

FOLLOW ME, AND I WILL MAKE YOU

Jesus instructed his disciples to follow him so that he could make them soul winners. There is a distinction between leading youth to our youth ministries and leading youth to Jesus Christ. The latter must be our focus. Soul fishing is but the first half of a two-sided coin. On the other side of the evangelism coin is discipleship, which as I already mentioned is all about sharing God's Word with believers in order to grow them in Christian maturity. In other words, both evangelism and discipleship are essentially the same thing—sharing the gospel. The distinction between them, however, is who the gospel is being shared with. Soul fishing is sharing the gospel with the lost to draw them to Christ and discipleship is sharing the gospel with believers to mature them in Christ. I will talk more about discipleship in the next chapter.

As Jesus developed followers, he discipled them and taught them how to reach the lost simultaneously. Before beginning his public ministry, Jesus began his private ministry of maturing disciples who would become soul fishers. We do not have to wait until our youth get to a certain level in their faith walk before encouraging them to share the gospel with others. We can disciple them and allow them to share the good news as they are being discipled. Raising up strong teenage Christians begins with following Jesus. Jesus provides for us a four-step process he used to raise his disciples into apostles (those he would send out to win souls). We can use this process to raise youth into mature Christians. This process includes calling, coming, copying, and conversion.

JESUS CALLED THEM

Youth workers have to busy themselves with the work of calling young people to Christ. This includes things like inviting them to church, sharing our testimony with them, communicating the gospel message frequently, bringing them to church or youth ministry events, and making sure that everything we do allows space to give an invitation for them to come to Jesus. Matthew 4:19 shows us that the first part of Jesus' training of disciples for soul fishing was to call them to himself. The text begins by saying, "Jesus called out to them." Jesus did not wait for potential students to come to him. He went out and decided to call people as pupil apprentices in the kingdom of God. The term *disciple* means a student, follower, apprentice, or simply one who learns from a leader. What were they learning? How to fish for souls. Jesus did not just sit around and wait for people to come and learn without taking the time to go out and call them to come to him. In the same sense, we can't just wait for youth to come, we have to go out and call them.

Soul fishing begins with a willingness to go where young people are and call them to Christ. It is okay to invite youth to church and it is okay to go to young people, but it is also crucial to let them know that God their Creator has a plan for their lives and he is calling them to himself. It is essentially our duty to extend the invitation to young people to come to Jesus not just the church. This is what many call relational evangelism. Relational evangelism is the type of soul fishing that invests time and is patient with an individual's process of accepting Christ as Lord and Savior. Relational evangelism begins with building our personal relationship with God, which will flow into our relationships with other people. It is important to understand that evangelism is verbal as well as non-verbal. God can and does use our lifestyle to lead people to Christ. Youth who we build relationships with hear what we say, but they also watch how we live. Remember Christians are like living epistles to be read by others. We should share the good news verbally to young people around us, but we also have to live a life that inspires youth to come to Christ.

THEY CAME TO CHRIST

Christ did even more with those who responded and came to him. The next step of Jesus' process in training his disciples for soul fishing was to devote time and attention to those who came to him. For the next three years, Jesus would spend time discipling those who came to him and preparing them to carry on his work once he left. We cannot train young people who do not answer the call to come to Jesus. While there is nothing wrong with pursuing young people, we must be careful not to invest too much time chasing those who are not ready to surrender to God that we lack time for those who have. We do not want to neglect or minimize the response of youth who have come to Jesus. Before I move on, I want to make sure that we understand coming to Jesus does not always mean conversion. It often means moving closer to him but not necessarily closing the deal with a confession of faith. Therefore, we can benefit from watching those who faithfully attend youth events and meet them where they are in their journey toward God.

It is helpful for youth leaders to take note of the youth who are coming around and discern whether they are coming for Jesus. Are they coming out of curiosity? Are they coming to ask questions? Are they sticking around after service concludes while everyone else is leaving? If this is the case, usually they are coming to get closer or at least seeking further direction. Youth who are coming to spiritual things and participating in the things of God ought not be overlooked, unnoticed, ignored, or more specifically, despised. Youth who are faithful to come should be faithfully invested in. When we recognize who is responding to the call to come to Jesus, it is time to invest more in helping them learn how to follow Jesus and become more like Jesus.

THEY COPIED CHRIST

Copying Christ means to imitate or become like him. Becoming fishers of people requires following, and following requires leadership. We cannot follow unless someone is leading. We see a cause-and-effect relationship in Jesus' statement in Matthew 4:19 (NASB). Jesus says, "Follow Me and I will make you . . ." Jesus' training was not a bunch of rules, strategies, and methods, but was simply get close to me, walk with me, and by doing so, I will teach and show you how to become like me and fish for souls. In other words, copy my life.

Only those who responded to the invitation to come were fortunate enough to be able to follow Jesus. By the command "follow me," Jesus meant to mimic, impersonate, copy, or repeat what is instructed or modeled by him. For the disciples this involved following Jesus' teaching as well as following the examples he modeled in his life. This is our work as youth leaders, to give direction, instruction, and examples to our youth on how to copy Jesus and become more like him. Though this may seem like the discipleship part of the two-sided coin I mentioned earlier, it is a discipleship process for the training of evangelism.

Paul said, "Follow me as I follow Christ" (1 Corinthians 11:1 KJV). What Paul was conveying to the church in Corinth was to follow his example because it was a result of him following Jesus' example. Teaching young people to follow Jesus is a process of show and tell. Both are equally important, and youth leaders cannot expect for youth to be serious about following Jesus if they are only instructing them but not actually living out what they are instructing. Young people need to see the example, work, and effort that goes into our following Jesus, but they also need to hear how Jesus instructs us to live in his Word. It must be both—hear it taught and see it modeled. As youth follow the examples of workers without knowing God's Word, they are still following Jesus because that is what we are doing as we lead them. This will require hard committed work, but it will pay off if we remain faithful and committed to invest in our young people. It is the following or copying of Christ that leads to our conversion in Christ.

THEY CONVERTED TO CHRIST

The disciples of Jesus were all in. They left their occupations and gave their entire lives to following Jesus. The fourth and final step in Jesus' process to train soul fishers is more of a result of the first three steps than a new step toward him. What we are looking for as we labor in youth ministry is the conversion of young people. What this means is for young people to go beyond being seekers or participants in the youth ministry to making a public and dedicated decision to surrender their lives to Christ. When young people are 100 percent committed to Jesus and decide to give all of their efforts to following him, this is what conversion looks like.

In Jesus' last statement in Matthew 4:19 (NLT), he said to the disciples who followed him, "I will show you how to fish for people." This is the end game and the purpose of soul fishing, that people come to Jesus and commit their lives to him while helping others do the same. This is the mission of Matthew 28:18-20 to make disciples of all people. The fruit of soul fishing among youth is the commitment of youth to soul fish for others. Youth who are sold out for Jesus and committed to his mission represent what true youth ministry is all about, recognizing and harvesting fruit for the kingdom of God.

GROWING YOUTH MINISTRY THROUGH EVANGELISM

During the week following Christmas in 1994, students in Chicago public schools went on winter break. During this time the youth ministry of the Salem Baptist Church of Chicago went on what we called "Evangelism Invasions," and this one was a mission trip to Atlanta. All of the youth paid for their own trip, and we fasted and prayed for six weeks in preparation. We would be in Atlanta for one week witnessing to the residents of a major urban American city. The goal of the trip was to lead one thousand people to faith in Christ. About sixty youth and around fifteen youth workers attended. This was our first out of state evangelism event for the entire youth ministry, and God used us tremendously.

As teenagers, following our youth leaders helped us to build a culture of evangelism among the youth. Although I already lived my personal life as an evangelist, I was able to grow in my knowledge of ways to engage and reach people for Jesus. We could be going to a meeting at a public school, and Pastor Carey would show me how to share my faith with a maintenance worker at the school. The next time we went somewhere, I would be the one to share my faith and the gospel with someone else. We talked about witnessing, how to witness, and its importance all the time. Every ministry meeting and event, whether formal or informal, a presentation of the gospel was given along with an invitation to come to Christ. This youth ministry showed and told young people how to lead people to faith.

When we went on the Evangelism Invasion trip in the winter of 1994, we brought our youth choir, our youth rappers, step dancers, theatrical troop, youth with powerful testimonies to share, and whatever else youth had to offer. In less than eight days, more than 1,200 souls placed their faith in Christ. I was about twenty years old at the time, and God used me alone to share the gospel and lead over one hundred people to faith in just one day. The youth used their skills to share the gospel everywhere we went in Atlanta. Some of the teens knew sign language and one of them led a group of hearing-impaired young people to faith in Christ. Some were fluent in Spanish and led a group of Spanish speaking youth to faith in Christ.

Some people try to delegitimize the type of evangelism that is not followed up by immediate discipleship. Their claim is that the salvation is not legit if they just utter a prayer to make Jesus Lord but are not being raised and discipled in your church. Paul explained to the Corinthian church that "neither [the person] who plants, nor [the person] who waters is anything, but only God, who makes things grow" (1 Corinthians 3:7). There are times when we lead people to Christ and are able to disciple them, and there are times when we lead people to Christ and have to encourage them to join a church and be discipled. But make no mistake about it, it is God who will cause them to grow, and it is God who we must pray and trust to do so.

The power was not in our method. The power of God was in the message, which means that we did not trust in strategies to evangelize or steps to lead people to faith, but we trusted that the gospel message alone was powerful enough to lead people to Christ. We did not sugarcoat the truth, but we were trained to be sensitive to where people were in their journey. Some people were not at a point in their life journey to consider Jesus, and we had to respect that and move out of the way. Some people were in crisis and looking for hope, and we would give them hope in Jesus. The manner of our engagement was important.

We found that the old saying was not always true, that if the hearers rejected the message, they were not rejecting you, but they were rejecting Christ. Some people were in fact rejecting us because we were too harsh in our manner of witness. We discovered that when our speech was harsh, insensitive, or disrespectful, people could actually be rejecting us not Jesus. We knew that those who won souls had to be wise. Being a young Christian at that time, you didn't want to miss church or any events because you wanted to be there to witness the power of Christ. We have seen people bring guns to the altar in worship and repentance, others would renounce their gang affiliation publicly, youth would testify before other youth that they were living a celibate life for God. On a weekly basis we witnessed the power of God to deliver our youth from many of the wiles that their peers were being consumed by.

SOUL FISHING IN OUR PERSONAL LIVES

The day following the shutting down of What's Poppin strip club that we prayed out of business, one of my rap partners, Michael D. Thomas, now pastor of Radiant Covenant Church in Seattle, was saddened that he missed the event. So the next day, Mike and I went back to see if the club was still closed, and it was. Mike was about eighteen years old, and I was about twenty-two, and we were saddened that we were not able to do ministry there because they were closed. We got out of our car and prayed that God would keep the club closed and then we got back into the car to go home.

While traveling home, we saw what appeared to be a mentally disturbed man in a violent rage, kicking parked cars, pushing over trash cans, talking to himself, and yelling out profanities. Mike and I looked at each other immediately recognizing that this was our ministry opportunity. Now, I know that many youth ministries would not advise young people to engage in what we were getting ready to do. Some would say that is not your area, and this person needs clinical help, but we saw it as the demonic possession of a soul that Christ had the power to set free. I want to be clear that mental illness is real and not always a result of demonic possession, but some conditions actually are. I do not share this story to encourage anyone to do what we did. We were led by the Spirit of God and were close enough to God at the time to hear his voice clearly. We believe that this mental disturbance was spiritual, and we addressed it as such.

We drove a couple of blocks in front of the direction the man was traveling, and we parked the car illegally with the back of it sticking out into the street. We hopped out of the car yelling out to the man, "Can we talk to you? Hey bro, what's wrong? Hey man, I got something to say to you." We followed the man about four blocks as he ignored us, then he abruptly turned around and yelled out, "Leave me alone." Mike and I recognized this as a frequent response of demons in the Scriptures that did not want to be cast out. Luke 4 is one example: "In the synagogue there was a man, which had a spirit of an unclean devil, and cried out with a loud voice, saying, Let us alone; what have we to do with thee, thou Jesus of Nazareth? Art thou come to destroy us? I know thee who thou art; the Holy One of God" (Luke 4:33-34 KJV). We see a similar response from one who was tormented with demons in Mark 5 just before Jesus cast the demons out of a man into a herd of pigs (Mark 5:1-16). It was our study of the Bible as young men that prepared us to discern what was happening spiritually.

Mike began to ask the man what was wrong, and Mike started talking about how Jesus loved the man and could fix whatever he was going through. I chimed in affirming the gospel, sharing the ways Jesus changed our lives. Then I asked the man if he knew Jesus. As we dialogued with this man, it was as if he transformed from a seemingly demented man who couldn't comprehend or engage in rational conversation to a rational man no longer loud or violent. It wasn't long before we extended an invitation for him to give his life to Christ. He agreed, and I began to lead him in prayer to ask Jesus to save him and come into his life.

I asked the man to repeat a prayer of faith after me. When I said, "Jesus come in to my heart," immediately, his eyes turned red, the volume of his voice increased, and he pointed to Mike and yelled, "Come into his heart!" There was a demon at work in him trying to deceive us. Mike prayed and rebuked the demonic spirit and the man trembled while his eyes became white again and he eventually invited Jesus to come into his life and be his Lord. We hugged this man, prayed for this man, and watched this man who just fifteen minutes ago was talking to himself and kicking over trash cans, acting violently, but now was walking down the street with a smile on his face like a mentally stable man, clothed and in his right mind.

As Mike and I turned around to go back and get the car out of the street, there were about twelve teenagers who we did not notice following us as we pursued the demon-possessed man. They were just standing there. So, we began to minister to them as well, and since they were our peers, I did a freestyle (impromptu rap) that God gave me on the spot to share the gospel with them. They were blown away and said, "Wow, that was a dope verse" (a very good rap verse). They appreciated the art and then they all gathered with Mike and me in a circle to pray and give their lives to Jesus. Mike and I were walking back to the car on a spiritual high and saw a seemingly homeless man passing by. Not intending to minister to him, we just spoke to him as we passed by and said, "How are you doing?" His response was, "I am doing bad," then he began to cry uncontrollably.

Now Mike began to minister to this man. We then find out he was a backslidden preacher who at the time was homeless. He fell out with his family years before and refused to reconcile. We reasoned with him, and he took our paths crossing as a sign of God reaching out to him. This man repented of his sins, re-committed his life to Christ, reconciled with his family, and has been off of the streets ever since as far as we know. As young people, we were trained to fish for souls corporately with our church but also individually in our personal lives. The focus of evangelism and the need for it is what caused our youth ministry to grow and gain the respect of our church and other churches across the city of Chicago. We were young, but we were not babies. We had a lot to offer the church and the kingdom of God. Youth ministry is first about soul fishing, reaching, and leading youth to be witnesses for Christ, but on the other side of the same coin, it is all about the discipleship of youth to maturity in Christ.

A DEEPER DIVE

The following communications are intended for reflection in order to help reverse the lack of evangelism toward youth in the surrounding neighborhoods of our churches.

1. Planning activities to build relationships and support the lives of youth in the community is a great way to provide

alternatives from the support gang members offer them. What are some activities your church can create to provide alternatives for your youth in the neighborhood?

2. Identify your personal challenges to evangelizing youth or helping youth evangelize. What are some ways these challenges can be addressed?

3. How often does your ministry teach, train, and practice evangelism and outreach in your community?

7

DRIVING DISCIPLESHIP

You then, my child, be strengthened by the grace
that is in Christ Jesus, and what you have heard
from me in the presence of many witnesses
entrust to faithful [people], who will be able
to teach others also.

2 TIMOTHY 2:1-2 ESV

SOUL FISHING IS BUT ONE SIDE OF THE SAME COIN.
Discipleship is the other side. While evangelism emphasizes
reaching for and drawing youth to Christ, discipleship emphasizes raising and maturing youth in their relationship with him.
The foundation of youth ministry is about reaching youth and
raising them in the faith. If evangelism is the floor, then discipleship is the ceiling. Everything else we do is meant to serve
these goals. We lead, teach, preach, counsel, care, minister,
worship, study, and have concerts, games, fun times, events,

and all sorts of activities to help young people surrender their lives to Christ and grow in him. We do all that we do so that youth can grow in the grace and knowledge of Jesus.

The mission of youth ministry is the same as the mission for the church outlined in Matthew 28:19-20 when Jesus charged his disciples, "Therefore go and make disciples of all nations, baptizing them in the name of the Father and of the Son and of the Holy Spirit, and teaching them to obey everything I have commanded you. And surely I am with you always, to the very end of the age."

Jesus' marching orders to the church in his Great Commission are three-fold. First, as we go about our lives in this world, believers are to evangelize, drawing all people and nations to God. Secondly, our orders are to baptize those who come to faith that they may advertise their identity with Christ and his church. Once youth are brought to faith and committed to the church, the next part of the call is to make them disciples. This means we are to teach those who come to Christ to learn and live out his will. Jesus promises that if we are "teaching them to obey everything I have commanded," he will be with us until the end of the age. This is discipleship.

A disciple is a student or one who is a learner. The main work of youth ministry is teaching young people about Jesus and helping them to learn his Word and his will for their lives. Youth ministries are to reach the lost and make them disciples of Christ. Youth leaders ought to drive discipleship as one of the primary works in their youth ministry if they expect Jesus to be with them in their work. There are a lot of factors that will fight for the attention of youth pastors and leaders. This means we must make sure that we remain focused on the mission of discipleship without distraction.

MAINTAINING FOCUS

Many youth ministries today are focused on all sorts of things to build their ministries and keep youth occupied instead of seizing opportunities to build the youth and ministry through routine discipleship. Like adults, youth will not learn based on a once-a-week or twice-monthly sermon in youth church. There must be multiple opportunities outside of the Sunday service experience for youth to learn about Jesus and his teachings. I am not saying that making sure youth are occupied is not important because it is. I am not saying that entertaining youth and making sure they have fun should have no focus because it definitely should. What I am saying, however, is that for everything you offer to your youth, make sure that it is driving discipleship.

Those who are in urban youth ministry should not neglect any opportunity to share about Jesus with their students and to help those young people in the ministry grow in their knowledge of God and his Word. We have to faithfully drive discipleship because for every hour of teaching youth receive from us there are about fifteen hours of the contrary message they are receiving in the world. There are formal ways to disciple youth, and there are informal ways. Youth ministries should grow in practicing both. We can teach youth formally in Bible studies, church, discipleship classes, or anything advertised, but we can also disciple youth in informal ways. This is when youth don't even realize that's what you are doing.

One way we can informally disciple youth is through sports. At our church, we typically get a group to go out and play basketball with other youth in the community. After playing we'd sit around and talk about Scripture and teaching from the

Bible. Other times we can go out for coffee or lunch and talk about all sorts of things and bring up Scripture as it addresses the topics we were discussing. Discipleship can happen anywhere and almost any way, but if we understand our mission to make disciples, we must remain focused on our assignment from God.

THE FRUIT OF DISCIPLESHIP

Pastor Carey was intentional in the discipleship of youth in the community. He did not wait for them to come to church, he met them where they were and took the time to talk about God with them. Many youth who had come to faith on the streets but did not attend church had no excuse because we would disciple them right there on the street. I had invited Jesus into my heart long before surrendering my life to him. Right on the front porch where we sold drugs, Pastor Carey led me in a prayer of faith, but it took over three years of my relationship with Pastor Carey and his discipleship with me in the neighborhood before I truly came to faith in Jesus. By the time I was eighteen years old, I had been arrested countless times, often released before my family would even know I was locked up. I had a drug case pending, an assault case, unlawful use of a firearm, aggravated kidnapping, and armed robbery. I had an arresting officer I will call Officer Warren. He took things so personally and made sure every time that I got into trouble with the law, he would show up to put in a bad word about me and convince the judge to put me away for good.

At the time, I also had a probation officer by the name of Officer Riddle, who was one of the meanest and worst people I could have ever dealt with. Before this, he had my probation violated falsely, which added six more months to my house arrest.

On a particular day, I was in court to make a plea agreement for a robbery and aggravated kidnapping case. I had been robbed by a rival Vice Lord gang member for drugs and money, so we went out and caught up with one of them. We robbed him and attempted to snatch him off the streets for ransom. The only problem was that Officer Warren happened to be passing by and caught us. A few months later, I was in court getting ready to plead guilty for a fifteen-year sentence to avoid twenty or more.

The night before I would go to court, I had an experience with God. The Gangster Disciples in my hood threw a going away party for me before I would have to turn myself in the next day. This party is where God opened my eyes to see that this was not about me. I witnessed close friends trying to get with my girlfriend before my eyes and acting like I was already in prison. I left the party before I did anything to get into more trouble, and I went to get very high on drugs, but somehow no matter how many drugs I did, I could not get high. When I looked at myself in the mirror, I appeared to look like a demon. A voice in my head said, "Look at yourself. You threw away your life for people who don't even care about you." The last time I stood before Judge John E. Morrisey, he told me that if I came before him again for any crime, he would make sure my bond was so high that Donald Trump would not be able to pay it. I was only eighteen and about to spend fifteen years in prison.

This is when the years of Pastor Carey's discipleship began to work in me. I heard about Jesus, and the gospel had been preached to me many times in the neighborhood. I prayed for God to save me, but I didn't really know if he was there. I was agnostic and had no real evidence that God existed, but at this moment I hoped that he did. I had this hope because I knew that it would take supernatural intervention to change my circumstances. I began to talk into the air and said,

If there is a God up there, please show me that you are real. If you exist, I will change my life and live for you. I am going to prove it tomorrow when I go to prison, and I will not claim my gang. I am going to read the Bible every day and to the best of my ability live by it. If you do not get me out of prison in five years or less, no one will ever be able to convince me that God exists.

When I went to court the next day Judge Morrisey was not there. Instead, there was a female judge who was giving out excessive sentences for the most menial offenses. I knew I was getting ready to be slammed, but when I stood before the judge, she asked for the arresting officer in the case. Officer Warren was nowhere to be found. Now this man made sure that he came to court appearances for cases he was not involved in just to put me away, but on the day of my plea agreement, he was not in court for his own case. The judge then called for the probation officer, and to my surprise, Officer Riddle was not there. Neither was the victim. This could not be a coincidence; it was a miracle.

The judge was so frustrated with the state that she lessened my charge from armed robbery and aggravated kidnapping (which are ineligible for probation) to a simple robbery. My sentence was one year of house arrest, three years of probation, and three hundred hours of community service at a church. I didn't have to go to prison at all. God had answered my prayer and showed me that he was real. He didn't wait for me to get in prison to prove my loyalty, he showed me that he could free me from prison altogether and my life changed from that moment. Suddenly, I was afraid because I was aware that God was real and that he knew all and saw all things, and he was nothing to play with. Those years of Pastor Carey talking about God with me, doing discipleship with me when I didn't even realize it, led me to lean on God when I was at the bottom of my rope. I surrendered all to God and committed to living for him for the rest of my life.

CREATING A CULTURE OF DISCIPLESHIP

From 1990 to 1998, the Salem Baptist Church of Chicago grew from a little more than two hundred to over 25,000 members mostly made up of people who had never been part of a church before. The secret to the spiritual and numeric growth of Salem was a culture of strong discipleship. Pastor James T. Meeks pushed the importance of discipleship in every aspect of the church, and it flowed down into youth ministry under Pastor Harvey Carey's tenure. Salem had the largest Sunday school attendance in the entire state of Illinois. People learned and grew in their faith through powerful teachers who were disciples and empowered to teach in the ministry. On the Monday that I returned from court, I had not heard from Pastor Carey for months and he happened to call my mother's house while I was there. I told him what God had done for me in court and he said, "That it is wonderful because I am calling you because God had you on my heart to attend a men's retreat at our church." I really wanted to attend this time. I had questions, but I was on house arrest. However, Pastor Carey got the information of the authorities who then permitted him to take me for the weekend.

My commitment to God was strengthened at this retreat, and I did my three hundred hours of community service eight hours a day and five days a week at the Salem Baptist Church afterwards. Every morning when I came for community services, the maintenance men would pray with me and lead worship and devotional before we would work and clean the church—good men such as Lee Crowder, Joseph Murphy, and Rev. Dearal Jordan, who was the children's pastor and building and grounds supervisor. Others helped me to see that God saves even the worst of sinners. I was hired as a maintenance man after I completed my community services, and these men thoroughly discipled and nurtured me in my faith. I grew because of the maintenance workers seeing the value of a young man and pouring into me as a Christian. They didn't see me as a criminal doing community service but a young man with potential for God's kingdom.

This church created a culture of discipleship, but the youth ministry created its own culture of discipleship as well. My world was different now. I gave up cigarettes, alcohol, drugs, and sex, and when the youth of Salem that had known me as a vicious gangster on the streets saw my transformation, it helped other youth to see the power of God and become more committed. We were proud to be enlightened and God-fearing teenagers. God was at work before our very eyes. Often the most influential factor in the transformation of youth is youth themselves. God was using us to help youth who were straddling the fence to move their commitment 100 percent to Christ.

Popularity and large numbers alone are but a façade. The real power is in the spiritual transformation of lives yielded through dedicated discipleship. Our youth created a culture of studying the Bible and teaching other teenagers how to study the Bible.

Youth began doing their own Bible studies at home with family members who did not go to church. As a result, the family members of these teens started attending Salem as well. As the youth ministry grew so did the church. Everyone benefited from what God was doing among the youth. We also had youth start Bible Clubs in their high schools, and these schools all across the city had teenagers from our church and others teaching the Bible and doing discipleship with their peers. Discipleship will be valued among the youth when youth workers value discipleship in their practice of youth ministry.

Youth pastors can help create a culture of discipleship by constantly and consistently casting vision around the work of discipleship. We can allow youth to teach and encourage them to have their own Bible studies. It is helpful when we help them to understand that they do not have to know everything in the Bible in order to teach it. All they have to do is know what someone else does not. Workers can let youth share stories about discipleship in their corporate worship gatherings. What is mentioned and celebrated will become valued. However, youth pastors cannot create a culture of discipleship alone. They can only lead people toward discipleship. It will take a remnant of members to cultivate a culture of discipleship. If you are leading a youth ministry as a director or youth minister, you have to push those around you to execute discipleship in their ministry to and through young people. Persistence in Jesus' plan is what produces fruit.

FOLLOWING THE MASTER'S PLAN

In his book *The Master Plan of Evangelism*, former professor of discipleship and evangelism at Gordon-Conwell Theological Seminary Robert Coleman looks to Jesus as the model for evangelism and discipleship in our churches. He asserts that Jesus used a strategy of investing most of his time in developing the few for the impact of the many. Coleman concludes that Jesus chose twelve who would follow him the closest, and he spent the majority of his time teaching and modeling the principles of the kingdom with them. Jesus invested time in discipleship with the Twelve because they were being prepared to continue Jesus' work once he returned to the Father. Coleman emphasized the fact that Jesus called trustworthy disciples to whom he could delegate the work of the ministry when his time was up. Our ministry to and through young people will be effective if we follow Jesus' model. Jesus identified and led three distinct groups to disciple. Many refer to this as the 3-12-72 Principle.

Although the main group of disciples focused on in the New Testament are the Twelve Jesus called to follow him, there are glimpses of these three groups. In Luke 10:1-12, Jesus sends out seventy-two of his disciples to minister in the towns. This is how we know Jesus had more than merely twelve disciples he taught, engaged, and spent time with. In Matthew 4, Jesus called the Twelve who would become apostles and later gave them power and authority as he sent them out to heal disease and sickness among the people (Matthew 10:1-15). In Matthew 10:8, Jesus told them to "heal the sick, raise the dead, cleanse those who have leprosy, drive out demons. Freely you have received; freely give." Jesus also had a smaller group of three from the Twelve. They were Peter, James, and John who would be his inner circle and leaders among the Twelve. They experienced and were exposed to things that the other disciples were not. They witnessed the transfiguration of Christ on the holy mountain. They were closest to Jesus in his hour of trial at

Gethsemane, and they were the only ones permitted in the room when Jesus raised Jairus' daughter from death. Peter, James, and John were privileged to have access to Jesus' work that others did not.

Jesus also did discipleship with the seventy-two differently from the way he did with the Twelve, and he did discipleship with the three in a way that was distinct from how he discipled the Twelve and seventy-two. The larger the crowd the less time and access Jesus gave them. Youth pastors and leaders will have to disciple both large groups and smaller groups, which will require being selective and giving most of their time to youth who stand out as faithful and obedient candidates. Allow these to be close enough to see the difficulties of ministry and the less glamorous parts of the work and use these scenarios as teachable moments for those who will become leaders who could be sent out later. If you follow the master's plan, you will not go wrong.

EDUCATE AND DEMONSTRATE

Like evangelism, discipleship must be show and tell. Good discipleship educates but also demonstrates how to follow Christ. Jesus not only taught but showed his disciples how to disciple others. For example, in John 13:15-17 Jesus declared, "I have set you an example that you should do as I have done for you. Very truly I tell you, no servant is greater than his master, nor is a messenger greater than the one who sent him. Now that you know these things, you will be blessed if you do them." Jesus is saying I have shown you what to do, therefore, do as you have seen me do. Jesus sets an example of kingdom leadership by washing the feet of his disciples. He wanted them to know that ministry requires humility and God's people must be willing to do whatever is needed to serve others.

Youth ministry is not lower level work, it is a work of God. Some feel you are not a real pastor until you serve as a senior or associate pastor in an adult congregation. I caution young leaders against thinking this way. Leading a youth ministry for the long haul will grow and equip you for the pastorate like little else can. Your approach to becoming a youth pastor should start with questions like, "Is this what God is calling me to do?" Not, "Is this a way for me to become part of the staff and do something else in a year or two?"

We need youth leaders to work hard on educating (teaching) and demonstrating (modeling) to young disciples how to follow Christ. Like Jesus, Paul taught and told his students how to minister. In 2 Timothy 2:1-2, Paul tells his young disciple, Timothy, "You then, my son, be strong in the grace that is in Christ Jesus. And the things you have heard me say in the presence of many witnesses entrust to reliable people who will also be qualified to teach others." As he did discipleship with a young Christian, Paul wanted to ensure that the things he told Timothy would not only be remembered and obeyed by him but taught to others.

Like Jesus' master plan, Paul urged Timothy to be selective about who he would give the majority of his time and attention to. Timothy was told to give this time to faithful people who would be able to teach others. Identifying youth who are not just disciples but also able to do discipleship with other youth is an essential part of developing a robust youth ministry. How can we identify those young people who can do discipleship? They are usually already natural leaders. Those who have influence in the lives of other youth and those who have interest in the Word of God should be utilized.

Identifying youth who are not just disciples, but able to do discipleship with other youth is an essential part of developing a robust youth ministry.

Youth workers can come up with creative ways to draw youth into discipleship opportunities at the church. Allowing youth to use their gifts in discipleship is always a draw. For instance, for the young person who likes to rap, they can be given a character or a passage in Scripture to write a rap about. This will give them inspiration but also allow them to take the study seriously because it is tied to their art. Some youths are not afraid to be front and center or to speak before crowds. These are young people we can invest time in discipling and preparing them to disciple others.

Driving discipleship is foundational to a thriving youth ministry, much of everything else is cosmetic. Faithfulness in discipleship will always be productive, but discipleship doesn't have to look the same. Youth can do discipleship through creating biblically based poems, sketching artwork, even planning trivia games for prizes. The idea in youth ministry is fun and creativity. We will not know when the fruit of discipleship will appear, but if we are faithful in listening and watching, we have to be faithful in showing and telling and know that God will bring forth fruit in his season, not our own.

A DEEPER DIVE

The following communications are intended for reflection in order to help reverse the lack of persistent discipleship of youth in our churches.

Training youth to disciple youth is a powerful way to create a culture of discipleship in your youth ministry. Often the most impactful discipleship is done outside of structured youth programming like youth church, Bible study, and Sunday school.

1. In what ways can you take youth deeper in their walk of learning and teaching God's Word?

2. What can your church do to drive discipleship among the teenage population in general?

3. Can you identify fruit in the lives of teenagers being discipled at your church? What are some ways you can encourage and celebrate them publicly to draw attention to it?

8

THE LANGUAGE
OF LOVE

A new command I give you: Love one another.
As I have loved you, so you must love one
another. By this everyone will know that you
are my disciples, if you love one another.

JOHN 13:34-35

HUMANITY THRIVES ON LOVE. The absence of love or feeling the absence of love can cause one despair and a desire to no longer live. Everyone wants to feel and experience love. Love makes life worth living and causes humanity to flourish. Love is one of those virtues that is easier to recognize than it is to describe. You may not be able to define it in depth but when you see, feel, or experience love you know exactly what it is. As a child growing up in the Roseland community on the south side of Chicago, I experienced love from my family, friends, and siblings, but as I began to experience the world on my own, I encountered a lot of hatred. A five-year-old child is not ready for the ugliness that young Black inner-city youth inevitably encounter in their communities. I would constantly be beaten up, jumped on, bullied, talked about, called out by my name, have things taken from me, and made fun of for just about anything. From the types of clothes that I wore to the brand of shoes I had on, to the area I lived in, to the color of my skin, hatred hardened me.

My experience of hatred led me to a perverted way of understanding love. Racism, bigotry, and prejudice discrimination affect minorities beginning at young ages. As a child, I learned that things were different for Black people. I grew up in a community that was predominantly White, but by the time I was nine or ten years old, most of the White people moved away. One of my best friends was a White kid name Billy. We played together every day, and even though I was a child, probably five or six years old, I could tell something was off with the behavior of his parents.

First thing every morning, whichever one of us woke up first would come to the other's house to play. Sometimes I went to get Billy and sometimes he came to get me. But one morning when I went to Billy's house, they were gone. The curtains were removed, and there was no furniture in the house. I learned that Billy's family moved during the night while we were asleep because they did not want to live in a neighborhood with Black people. White flight was in full effect. Not only did White neighbors move, but so did White businesses, causing the property value to decrease and leading to a decline in the community. Although this book is not about social justice, I do want to mention that institutional racism, real estate red lining, a perpetuation of the school-to-prison pipeline, and other factors have contributed to a lot of the conditions that urban minorities live in and the traumatrigenic nature of these communities our youth have to navigate.

Every community needs resources. Business owners need capital and loans to support the success of their businesses and contribute to the well-being of a community. However, there is often a disproportionate imbalance between what Black business owners experience from lenders and what White business owners experience. Racism, discrimination, poverty, and social trauma were felt realities for me and many other minorities even at a young age. For me, kindergarten was a true culture shock. I had to learn how to grow up and get tough really quick. When I learned how to fight back, it showed me that people were quick to bother those who seemed weak but thought twice about those who would defend themselves or retaliate. This caused me to become more vicious and brutal. Violence became a preemptive way to safeguard myself from victimization. I found that, win or lose, you better fight back or it could cause others to attack you.

In many urban low-income communities, it is survival of the fittest. My neighborhood was occupied by the Disciples gang. Back then everyone was called Disciples, but later on other factions under the Disciples umbrella emerged. There were Gangster Disciples, Black Disciples, and Black Gangster Disciples. I chose to be what my friends and my community were and did all I could to make a name for myself in the streets. We wanted to cause our enemies to think twice about starting problems with us. It was love for my gang and my set (street areas occupied by a particular gang faction) that fueled my way of life, but I would later find that my perception of love was obscured.

THE PERCEPTION OF LOVE

It was the perception of love that kept me loyal to the street code. It was my perception of love that would cause me to trust these guys and commit crimes and acts of violence for them. At the time I thought, these are the ones who are always there for me. They love me, and I love my neighborhood. These are the ones who make sure I eat when I am hungry and that I get money when I need it. When anyone bothers me, they are the ones there to make sure that the offenders pay for their actions. When you are young, these types of things are perceived as love, and you are willing to reciprocate for them what you perceive as love. Make no mistake about it, young people want to be loved, but like myself as a young man, many of them are confused on what real love is.

When I got to the bottom of my rope as a young man, I realized that their acts of violence did not reveal their love for me but only their love for violence. When I would get incarcerated, I began to realize they didn't love me, they only loved being gangsters. When they beat up someone, it wasn't out of love for me but out of their love for beating people up. When they would hang out and get high with me, it wasn't because they loved me. They just loved to hang out and get high.

Like many youth today, I had a false perception of love. It was the love of God at the time that changed me, though I could not put into words or understand it as God's love. A comparison between the acts of the boys in my hood and the church in our hood helped me to recognize real love, and after several years of fighting against that love, I finally surrendered my life to God. The love of God through his people changed my life forever.

Our young people need to feel, see, and touch true love.

Urban youth today are experiencing the same counterfeit love that led me and so many others astray when I was young, and the real love of God is still a transforming agent for even the seemingly toughest of young men and women. Our young people need to feel, see, and touch true love. Our young people need real love and not counterfeit love. The youth worker well equipped and experienced in all of the strategic approaches, methods, and remedies of youth ministry can be less effective than the uneducated committed worker who is driven by their love for God and young people. The love of God is among the most powerful resources of the church in the work of reaching, respecting, and raising strong young Christians. An effective means for influencing young people to follow God is an understanding of the power, command, and language of love.

THE POWER OF LOVE

Love is a powerful emotion. Love is a spiritual ethic. Love can be felt and experienced. Love is real as a noun but experienced as a verb. Love is an action word, powerful enough to cause one to give their life and also powerful enough to live life for another. Love can do a lot of things. It can be productive, it can be a means of healing, it can be encouragement, and it can change people. This is the power of love. Love is mentioned in hundreds of passages throughout the Bible and is one of the most declared values throughout the Old and New Testament Scriptures.

Many people understand love as something that you feel, but the Bible reveals love as something that is also done. There is a distinction between love and affection. Affection is a noun that refers to a feeling one has about something or someone. Affection is typically conditional. However, the Greek word used in the Bible to describe the love of God is *agapē*, and its verb form is from the same root, *agapaō*. Agape is unconditional love. This means that biblical love is a product of our affections as well as our actions, and it is a choice that is not based on conditions. This is the type of love that the youth in our congregations and communities need to experience.

The adolescent season is often a conflicted one. Youth feel like adults and want to make their own decisions and are often in conflict with adults and authority figures about their choices. When young people come to church, it is helpful for us to provide for them a unique experience from all other places they frequent. That experience ought to be filled with love. They ought to be able to feel it from the people they encounter in the parking lot to the affection given them in the foyer, to the worship service and beyond. Youth ministries can benefit from youth workers who are intentional about reflecting on ways to promote and distribute love toward their youth.

Our love for the young people under our care needs to be expressed not only in the church but outside of the church as well. All activities, meetings, and events with youth outside of the church need to be communicated with the church and authorized by the parents of the youth. In addition to this, be sure to have another youth worker or youth with you ensuring a safer community of at least three people. A sit down for coffee, a meal at McDonald's, a game of cards or chess, bowling, or a walk and talk in the neighborhood are all ways to subconsciously express your love to the youth you serve. Time outside of church says, this is about more than just church and that you care for them.

The Bible is clear that love is a powerful motivator, movement, and ministry of the Lord. Love can be one of the greatest impacts on the lives of your youth. Love is capable of accomplishing even what our skills and years of experience in youth ministry cannot. The apostle John tells us, "Whoever does not love does not know God, because God is love" (1 John 4:8). Knowing God, who is love, is what both enables and causes us to authentically love. In youth ministry, I would often help young ladies understand that when a boy says he loves you, he really can't love you until he knows God because God is love. Like boys, girls seek love as well, and because most females are more in touch with their feelings than most males, who seem to be more visually driven, our young ladies can benefit from guidance to safeguard them from divisive boys. However, many of us miss the opportunity to lead our young men to live a chaste life and guard themselves from the lures of young women.

Likewise, our young men are typically focused on love when it comes to leading our youth away from the dangers of gangs. However, many of our young ladies are heavily involved in gangs as well as drug abuse and drug dealing. This can also be to seek what is perceived as love from their peers, their personal love for money and narcotics, or just loving what the crowds love in order to fit in. Love draws us, and if the object of our love is wrong, we will be drawn to the wrong things. But as we personally experience the love of God, others can experience his love through our love toward them. First John 4:19 lets us know, "We love because [God] first loved us." This is why one of the greatest memory verses to give to our youth is John 3:16, which declares, "For God so loved the world that he gave his one and only Son, that whoever believes in him shall not perish but have eternal life." We have to help our youth (male and female) understand the difference between real and counterfeit love.

THE COMMAND TO LOVE

Sometimes serving urban youth is frustrating, and these youth can get under your skin. Youth can be difficult, disobedient, disrespectful, disengaged, and disappointing, but we have to love them the same way God loves us—unconditionally. Paul is reminding us to "do everything in love" in our youth ministry (1 Corinthians 16:14). This is a command. First John 4:7 says, "Let us love one another, for love comes from God. Everyone who loves has been born of God and knows God." The apostle Peter says, "Above all, love each other deeply, because love covers over a multitude of sins" (1 Peter 4:8).

The love of God through Jesus' sacrifice on the cross is what covered our sins and allows us to be in God's presence without condemnation. In the same way, we have to love the youth under our care in a way that covers their flaws, mistakes, and failures because that is how God loves us all. Proverbs 10:12 tells us, "Hatred stirs up conflict, but love covers over all wrongs." When youth make mistakes, and they will make many, this is an opportunity for us to help transform them by approaching them with love.

In my years of urban youth ministry, I have experienced some of the worst acts and treatments by youth. I have caught youth having sex in the church bathroom. I've dealt with youth attending church events while high on drugs. I have confronted youth and confiscated large amounts of drugs for distribution and even confiscated guns brought on the church premises. I have dealt with dishonest youth and youth in cycles of recidivism in the correctional system. I have experienced this and a whole lot more, but never did any young person under my care not know that I loved them mistakes and all.

One of the teens I took guns and drugs away from actually became a minister and graduated from the Moody Bible Institute about five years later. Love has a way of changing us. Paul's words in 2 Corinthians 5:14-15 say, "Christ's love compels us, because we are convinced that one died for all, and therefore all died. And he died for all, that those who live should no longer live for themselves but for him who died for them and was raised again." Love cannot be counterfeited, and it cannot be faked. Real love makes all the difference in the world. Love is a universal language, but please understand that we all experience and sense love in a variety of ways.

THE LOVE LANGUAGES

In 1992 the now world-renowned Dr. Gary Chapman published his life-changing book *The 5 Love Languages*.[1] Since then, it has been published in over fifty languages, sold over 14 million copies, and has been on the *New York Times* bestseller list.[2] For over forty years, Dr. Chapman was a clinical family counselor and noticed patterns in the way people felt and expressed love toward one another. This led to his writing of the book, which has helped countless families over the years both within and outside of the church. My wife and I first encountered *The 5 Love Languages* in the first few months of our marriage in 1996, and it has made a tremendous difference for us.

Chapman teaches that based on the various personalities of people in relationships, there are five distinct ways people feel loved by others and express their love to others. When we learn to recognize the ways that we feel loved and the ways we express our love, it helps us to communicate in ways that people can understand we are loving them. The love languages are ways of communicating love, but because some communicate love and understand love differently from others, there is room for miscommunication. In other words, just because one expresses their love to someone doesn't mean that their expression of love is seen as such by the recipient.

Chapman identifies the five love languages as words of affirmation, acts of service, receiving gifts, quality time, and physical touch. The love languages have not only helped my wife and I to cultivate our marriage for almost thirty years but also have been useful to me in youth ministry, marriage ministry, and premarital counseling. I have used the teachings of *The 5 Love Languages* for over twenty years now, and it has equipped couples with the tools to enable them to build strong marriages. The love languages can help equip parents to communicate love to their children and understand when their children are communicating love to them. The same is true with youth ministry. It is extremely helpful to observe how our youth receive and express love if we want them to recognize the love we are expressing toward them.

Allow me to explain how each of these five expressions is designed to speak love. The first thing we need to understand is that people often express their love in the same way they perceive being loved. In other words, a person who feels loved by affirming words will express their love to others by sharing words of affirmation. Now the challenge with this is that when a person who feels loved by receiving gifts is being loved through words of affirmation, even though they are being loved, they can still not feel loved. Children who feel loved by quality time will feel unloved when their father expresses his love by giving them gifts without spending time with them. A child who craves your time will not feel loved by your gifts. When we understand this, we can learn to communicate love in specific ways that the person will be able to feel loved by us. This is what we need to do with our young people.

Words of affirmation. This is when you express your love in words by affirming what you admire about someone. Words of affirmation like, "You are very intelligent," "I appreciate how helpful you are," "Darnell, I want you to know that I notice how faithful you have been in attending church," "Sheryl, God is really using you, and I am so proud of you," are all affirming of young people who feel loved when you use words to affirm them. Youth workers can be able to recognize youth who feel loved by words of affirmation when they see youth who express their affection through words or respond enthusiastically when you affirm the positive things that you see or sense in them through your words.

Acts of service. Love expressed through acts of service is when someone feels loved by things being done for them. For youth who love and feel love through acts of service, we express our love for them by performing acts to serve them. Some examples are helping youth with their homework, giving them a ride home from an activity, opening a door for them, or setting up an area in the church for them can all be acts of service that would help these youth feel loved. Youth who feel loved by acts of service will express their affection for us through their acts of service, and we can see it as their loving us back.

Receiving gifts. This love language expresses love and receives love by the giving of gifts. Some good examples of loving through gifts can be purchasing school supplies, giving out a bag of candy, or giving your youth a book or a gift card. These can all help them feel your love. For youth who feel loved through receiving gifts, it is not about the size of the gift but the thought that matters.

Quality time. The fourth love language is quality time, and it means just that—spending quality time with a person helping them feel loved and the person who feels loved when you spend quality time with them expresses their love for you when they are attempting to spend time with you. The youth who are continually asking you to do something with them, like play basketball, video games, attend a school event, or anything that allows you to be with them are expressing their love in their love language. It is important to recognize how huge it is that a young person would want to spend time with you. It is crucial to understand in real time that this young person is expressing love. They are saying, "I like you, and I feel treasured when you, a youth worker, will take the time to do something with me."

Physical touch. The fifth and final love language Chapman identifies is physical touch. This is when touch is identified as love and love is expressed through touch. This particular gift must be expressed with a little more caution. Some practitioners of youth ministry discourage touch for understandable reasons, like triggering uncomfortable or traumatic feelings for youth who have been victims of abuse or the potential for miscommunication of what a touch could mean. However, when done appropriately in the right way by people who have earned trust and are known by their youth, physical touch can do much for the edification of a young person who needs physical touch in order to feel loved.

For example, when I was a youth pastor at Oakdale Covenant Church in Chicago, some girls had experiences that made them uncomfortable with opening up to a male youth pastor. During this time, I had women youth workers give them extra attention and inform me on what I needed to know about them. But the way I carried myself, showed interest and concern for our youth, and taught them the Word addressing as many issues of life as I could, allowed these young ladies to be healed over time. There is not a time when I see them today that they don't get a huge hug from me and they understand exactly what it means—that I love them with the love of God.

Many of the young men and the young ladies felt loved through physical touch and all of our workers made sure that these youth knew they were loved. Recognizing youth who identify with love through touch is important because these are youth who will not truly feel loved without physical touch. They need assurance, they need to feel valued and loved. This is done in ways like a simple hug (a side hug is a safe start), a laying on of hands, a holding of hands in prayer, taps on the back, or anything that can assure them that you care for them. Once we know the love language of our youth, we have to be intentional about expressing our love in a language that they will understand.

Chapman's teaching on the five love languages can be revolutionary in your youth ministry. You can begin to recognize the love language of your youth by discerning the patterns of their love expressions. However, you can also be intentional and allow your staff and the youth in your ministry to take the love language test for themselves.[3] But I want to caution you that love, when not properly understood, can become perverted. People can express counterfeit love, and their actions that are not meant to express love can be falsely perceived as love. Godly discernment and cautionary discretion must be used.

THE LANGUAGE OF LOVE

While Chapman provides a resource for understanding love languages, we must also know that love is a language in and of itself. The language of love is universal to all people. Everyone needs love. Everyone responds to love. We can do more to influence spiritual growth in a young person by being loving to them than we can by almost anything else. The seemingly most difficult young person, the promiscuous teenager, the hardened gang banger, the young diva with an attitude, and the disrespectful youth can all be transformed by the language of love. In the discipleship and evangelistic outreach of youth, love will be one of your greatest gifts. First Corinthians 13:13 says, "And now these three remain: faith, hope and love. But the greatest of these is love." Wait a minute, love is greater than faith? Even hope? In what way? Well, first we must understand the difference between being greater than and being better than.

Paul is not saying that love is better than faith and hope. His point is love is greater. This means that love is bigger in the scheme of things. Both faith and hope are fueled by love. A person with faith in God but no love cannot exist. As was mentioned earlier, the Bible teaches us that a person who does not love does not know God because God is love (1 John 4:8). According to Galatians 5:22, "the fruit of the Spirit is love," then it is "joy, peace, patience, kindness, goodness, [and] faithfulness." Love plays a role in the gifts that God gives us that is greater than all of the other gifts. If you are incredibly gifted and you serve with your gifts in youth ministry but are not loving people, it means nothing. This is why Paul says, "If I have a faith that can move mountains, but do not have love, I am nothing" (1 Corinthians 13:2).

In the same way, there can be no true hope without love because we hope for what we desire and love. It is love that brings our faith and hope to life, and it is our love that can bring the faith and hope of the teenagers to life. Our faith is alive because God loved us first and his love gave fuel to our faith and hope. When we serve out of love, it is powerful and makes our ministry more impactful. Youth will respond to and grow in faith through a loving youth pastor and loving youth workers.

But it is not only Paul who places love as the greatest gift, Jesus does as well. When Jesus was asked what is the greatest of all God's commandments,

> Jesus answered, "The most important is, 'Hear, O Israel: The Lord our God, the Lord is one. And you shall love the Lord your God with all your heart and with all your soul and with all your mind and with all your strength.' The second is this: 'You shall love your neighbor as yourself.' There is no other commandment greater than these. (Mark 12:29-31 ESV)

Loving God and loving people is the principle behind all of the particular laws. The language of love then is the foundation of all ministry work. Jesus taught that there is no greater commandment than the command to love. God is love, and we are recognized as his people when we have love for one another. Love is an action perceived by how the recipient of love identifies love. Love is powerful, and it is not only commanded of God but is the greatest of all his commandments. The language of love is an important factor in our ministry with youth, and understanding how youth are loved helps us to speak their language. We need to love our youth, love our churches, love our community, love our pastors, love our workers, and love God because love never fails. May we love in word and deed as we lead our youth to maturity in Christ.

A DEEPER DIVE

The following communications are intended for reflection on ways to ensure our youth are experiencing the love of God through our ministries.

1. How can your understanding of the five love languages impact the way you do youth ministry at your church?

2. Can you identify youth in your ministry who feel unloved though you have engaged them in a loving manner? Are you able to identify their love language?

3. How might your understanding of the love languages help you to combat youth who are influenced by a perverted and false sense of love from figures in their community?

4. Can you identify youth in your ministry who are responding to the language of love? Are you noticing ways that their love is expressed to others in the ministry?

5. How can your ministry begin to reflect on ways to promote and distribute love toward your youth and identify and note their particular love languages?

PART THREE

THE NECESSITY OF WAR

9

TO THE CONGREGATION

*Even so the body is not made up
of one part but of many.*

1 CORINTHIANS 12:14

GROWING UP IN POVERTY is a battle in and of itself. Although much of my attention has been focused on the darkest issues of the inner city, there are families living in the same areas who are fighting their battles differently. Some youth battle through education, some battle through sports as a way to support their higher level education. Others are from families of blue-collar workers fighting to provide a better life for their children in the hood. All of the youth in the inner city are not fighting to survive on the other side of the law, many are fighting to stay away from the gangs and drugs. Along with those struggling with gangs and addictions, they need others to go to war with them in order to rise above the obstacles in their paths.

The need to teach youth and youth workers to war was a vital part of the youth ministry that nurtured my spiritual growth as a young man. Nothing just happens, which means if we want the realization of an idea to come to pass, we have to do the work to get it there. It is not an accident or a coincidence that a youth ministry is successful. Any successful youth ministry would have the same thing in common—they worked at it. At the Salem Baptist Church of Chicago, youth ministry grew to a weekly attendance of more than 1,500 youth, and dozens of ministers, pastors, and church leaders were produced from the youth who were a part of the youth group in the 1990s alone.

This ministry in a context of urban poverty produced many full-time ministry workers and others who didn't choose full-time ministry but decided to live out their faith in a variety of secular vocations such as attorneys, politicians, civic servants, teachers, professors, and more. It would be far from the truth to say that all of this just happened. No, we fought many battles to ensure that young people knew God and knew who they were in him. Youth ministry helped to get and keep youth on track to being productive members of society and the kingdom of God. We fought for youth to have space, to have opportunities, to be invested in, and to experience spiritual and social freedom. It was all intentional because everyone worked together to make sure the young people received the ministry and support they needed. At times it was a battle but a necessary fight that produced fruit. It is my prayer that this chapter will inspire and equip you to fight for the spiritual growth of the youth in your congregation and battle anything in the way of that goal.

YOUTH AND THE BATTLE FOR SOULS

In the mid-1990s, I saw an HBO documentary on the growing gang problem in Little Rock, Arkansas, called *Banging in Little Rock*.[1] Although they had different gangs than the ones we had in Chicago, they were very active and spreading death and destruction for the population of youth in the urban context of Little Rock. I showed the documentary to my youth pastor and as a result, we planned a mission trip to Little Rock to minister to the young people there.

Our youth had been equipped over the years to do ministry in dark and difficult settings. This is not because everyone identified with or were involved in the street life. In fact, many of the youth at Salem Baptist Church lived in suburban areas, did well in school, and stayed away from the negative elements of the streets. This is clear evidence that you do not have to be from the streets to reach the streets. Youth workers do not have to have personal experience with the trials youth in the streets wrestle with in order to engender change in the lives of these youth. Love and God's Word are enough in our battle to win their souls for God. Our church reached out to some of the congregations that were on the documentary and got the support of some of their locals to come to their town and into various venues to minister to their youth.

Our trip was planned to occur during the Christmas break, and we began fighting against the spiritual powers at work in Little Rock with over 100 youth and thirty-plus youth workers fasting and praying together in preparation for the trip. Once in Arkansas, we ministered in churches, schools, firehouse stations, massive shopping malls, outdoor urban communities, and any door God opened for us. However, one of the most powerful events to win souls to God occurred at a super-max prison called the Varner Unit in down state Arkansas. The men in this facility committed some of the most heinous crimes ever from rape, murder, and serial killings—they were all sent to the Varner Unit.

As we rode there on the two-hour trip, we worshiped, we prayed, we prepared, and finally we arrived. Once we reached the prison, the warden was very stern with rules. We could not look the inmates directly in their eyes, we could not shake their hands, we could not be closer than twenty feet to them. They warned us that at any moment they could shut our chapel service down and that the last group they had there was attacked by the inmates. None of this scared us. We knew God was with us, and we understood that it was all spiritual.

As we began to get off of the buses and bring in our sound system, the inmates in the upper-level cells began to expose themselves through the cells toward the girls who were with us. We could feel a dark demonic presence there. There was such a thick tension in the air. Pastor Carey told us to go back into the buses to pray, and we did. We prayed loud, we prayed fervently, we prayed in the Spirit, and we did spiritual warfare like our lives depended on it. Once we came into the unit and began the service, we started with a skit and our step dance group followed it. The men there seemed to be hardening themselves, but they were starting to loosen up.

Then I came up to share my testimony as a former certified gang member in Chicago, and as I spoke, I could see the whites of their eyes turning red and holding on to every single word. They understood the struggle and knew that it was authentic. They knew that I understood their world and that my homeboy Bo who rapped with me came from their world. They were able to hear and receive hope. Then our rap group, D.O.C. (Disciples Overcoming Corruption), performed a song titled "From Rags to Riches in Glory." This song was a testimony of how God got us out of physical and spiritual prison, but before we could finish the song, men began to burst out audibly and uncontrollably weeping and shouting at the top of their voices. Tears were flowing everywhere. Men didn't care how the other men saw them. Some even stood and lifted their hands to God in worship and prayer. At that moment Pastor Carey knew it was time to preach. They hung on to his every word and surrendered to the Spirit of God at work. This is what the world can't compete with, and this is what makes a real difference: the presence of God.

When I tell you there was not a dry eye in the place, believe me. Even the guards working there were crying. Pastor Carey shared the gospel and led these men to faith in Christ. Our youth began hugging these men, laying hands on them, and praying for them while leading them in the sinner's prayer. The corrections officers who were paid to watch these men also had their eyes closed asking Jesus to save them. It was so powerful. We were warned about looking into the inmate's eyes or getting too close, but those rules went out the door when the power of God filled that place. Some of our youth left their Bibles there with men who had no Bible to read.

As we left the place to go back to our buses, the same men who earlier exposed themselves through the cell doors to the girls were now holding their Bibles in the air through their cells and pointing up to God as we departed. All we could do when we got on that bus was cry overwhelmingly. This result did not happen by accident. It was spiritual warfare that set the stage for God's power to work unhindered by the dark forces at play, winning the souls of these inmates. I share this story to encourage the various members of our congregations to trust the potential of God in our youth to accomplish powerful exploits for his glory.

FIGHT THE POWER

In the fight for the lives of our youth, there are many types of battles. Sometimes we have to fight systems designed to marginalize and enslave them. At times we have to fight false narratives that brainwash others about who we are as urban minorities from the inner city. We have to fight for the wellbeing of our youth amongst the unique social issues they encounter. We have to fight the injustices that impact the lives of our youth, from discrimination in employment to legislation that leads to nonpunitive acts of police brutality, and the murder of unarmed Black men, and stop-and-frisk laws to infringe upon the civil rights of our teenagers. Life in urban America is impacting our youth in many ways, and we cannot let them fight these battles alone. Our congregations have to fight for their rights and for them to be supported in our churches. However, at the core of every battle, there is a spiritual component, and above all things, we must learn to commit to fighting the spiritual powers at work.

In Ephesians 6, Paul urges the church to stand. This means not to leave when the battle gets tough. Standing is not always easy. Many youth ministries struggle not because the youth are unfaithful, but because congregations who are called to serve the youth leave them to fend for themselves and they lack perseverance to remain committed to them. Youth ministry requires resilience. Youth ministry workers must stand even when it is hard. To stick with the ministry, even if you have to suffer blows to protect young people and allow them to grow. To stand means to maintain the work we are doing for our youth. When we feel like fleeing, that is really the time when we need to fight harder. Powers are coming against our young people that they are not yet mature enough to handle alone, so every part of the congregation must come alongside the young to help see them through. Standing with and for them no matter what is a display of our unconditional love.

THE BODY OF CHRIST

Although the primary audience I am seeking to reach through this book is practitioners of Christian ministry with youth, much of what is discussed is applicable to a large array of congregations and church members. Not only can those who serve low-income inner-city churches benefit from valuing the youth in urban settings, but many congregations in the suburbs outside of the city with a heart for transformation can get involved with the work of reaching and raising urban youth in the faith. Every local church is an assembly of God's people from many walks of life. Our congregations are made up of a variety of people, gifts, resources, and skillsets. Many congregations in different communities are called to God's mission work in the inner city as well.

We all have different parts to play and gifts to contribute, but we must be unified for the edification of the entire body, teenagers included. The question is how can the congregation work together to help their younger members? At-risk-youth, teenage new believers, unchurched youth, leaders in development, high school students, and student athletes are in our congregations and can utilize this information to value the youth in the church.

One of the most used metaphors to describe the church is "the body of Christ." This term has a twofold meaning. On the one hand, the church represents Christ Jesus on earth (as his body), and Jesus is the head who uses his people to walk, talk, teach, reach, preach, serve, heal, and do his work on earth. On the other hand, the body of Christ is a metaphor to describe the way that God's people are connected and work together for the cause of Christ. That is, the congregation is a body made up of many parts working together.

There are diverse people, diverse generations, genders, classes, ethnicities, and contexts who all have different gifts meant to work together for the cause of the entire church. Believers are members of Jesus and members of one another in the same way the parts of a human body are connected and must work together to accomplish things. The hand has to work with the arm, the legs have to work with the feet, and the feet move the body to a particular place to speak but must depend upon the mouth and the tongue to speak once there. In the same way, the members of our congregations have a role to play in helping youth to get where God is calling them to be. When we come together to battle for our youth, they are better positioned to become who God is calling them to be.

TO THE PARENTS

To the parents of teenage children in our congregations, I know the struggle and the difficulties of raising children. As my wife and I have raised our children to adulthood together, I struggle to see how single parents are raising multiple children alone. I understand that many children in the urban context are being raised by their grandparents, a sibling, or another guardian for various reasons. I also know the difficulty of keeping our youth on the right track in urban environments. This is one of the reasons I believe our congregations should serve as a support system for the families in our communities.

I want to encourage parents of teenagers to see the importance of partnership with the congregation in the development of your child or children. If there is no father in the home, there are men in the church. Many fathers are single parents as well, which is why it is helpful to know that there are women in the church to help with their daughters. If you have no car to get the youth to events, someone at the church should be able to help. If there are problems too big to tackle alone, you should be able to seek support from the congregation.

The adolescent years are the most formidable years for your children and will ultimately set the foundation for who they will become in life. It is good for parents in the congregation to have the support of a church to come alongside them help meet the needs of their children. However, both sides have to do their parts together. No matter how much the church puts together for youth and no matter how involved your children are, remember that God ultimately holds the parent responsible for raising the children in the faith. No parent can expect to merely give their child to the church and wait for the church to give them back changed and transformed. Parents have to do their part at home and work with the youth ministry as they do their part at church. Parents play an extremely vital role not only in the lives of their teens but also in the youth ministry as a whole. As a parent in the congregation, your support is needed not just when your child is in their season of youth but also for youth who need support from the church even after you have raised your children.

Parents who take responsibility for the spiritual development of their children ought to make sure that their children attend church and the events and activities the church provides for them. It sounds simple and easy, but believe me, at times it can be a fight. Often, it is a fight for parents to find time to get youth to events at the church. Sometimes it is a fight to find time for youth to attend church events because their schedules are filled with outside extracurricular activities. Though many of these events have no spiritual significance, they can be helpful in the development of the student. However, when it takes away time for your child to worship, learn the Scriptures, and work on aligning their priorities with God's, these activities can become a distraction and a tool for the enemy to lead your children astray.

As parents we must fight to make time for our children to be involved in the church. We cannot wait for them to get into trouble before we get them involved in the church, and we cannot wait until we have time in our schedules. We must make time for their spiritual growth—for church attendance, discipleship, Bible study, and the things that have spiritual and eternal significance in their lives. Raising children in the church requires focus, dedication, and sometimes sacrificing the things they want to do for the things that they need to do. However, youth who attend church with parents who do not attend will have even a harder time staying grounded. The good news is that normally when the church disciples youth who attend church on their own, it usually leads to their parents becoming part of the church as well. In this case the youth are actually leading their parents.

Raising children is the primary responsibility of their parents, however, God never intended for it to be done outside of partnership with the family of God, the church. Parents have to be the primary spiritual leader in the lives of their children and parents have to fight to make sure their children are involved in the church, but parents are also responsible for working with the church in the development of the spiritual lives of their children. This means being involved. Here are a few ways parents can get involved.

Know the youth workers. Parents ought to know the youth pastor or director if there is one, and the youth pastor or director needs to know the parents. The same is true for Sunday school teachers, discipleship classes, and youth programming directors. It is important to be familiar with the youth workers, and when there are events or times when the parents are invited, parents must fight to be there. This is not only important for the parents but also for the ministry and the youth who are a part of it. The parent's presence supports the youth and the youth workers, and being present allow parents to see what their children are obtaining from church.

Know the youth work. Even more important than knowing the youth workers is making sure to know what is happening in youth church and programming, and reinforcing it rather than contradicting it. Again, I know this is a fight. If the communication is not good at church or a parent finds themselves clueless about what is going on, it is worth having a conversation with youth leaders to come up with a communication system that works for you. Single parents, parents without a car, and parents with multiple children need to know what is happening, and fees for retreats and events may need to be discounted or subsidized for single parents with multiple children. Last-minute communication with such parents may cause their child to miss out on something.

Talk about youth work. Another way a parent can support the ministry for their youth is by discussing what is going on in youth ministry with their children. If the youth ministry is teaching about sexual purity, not only should a parent know but it also creates opportunity for parents' input. More than that, discussing what's happening in youth church allows parents to discern how their child is experiencing the youth ministry.

Battling the powers at work against our youth is the responsibility of everyone in the congregation.

Fight for your child(ren). Raising youth is a battle, and though it should be a given, I don't want to assume that all parents are praying for their children or their youth ministry. Battling the powers at work against our youth is the responsibility of everyone in the congregation. Parents have to fight for their children to be who God has called them to be as well. The life we live in front of the youth is influential whether we recognize it or not. This is important for our development but also for the youth. It does not matter if we as parents make mistakes as long as we can acknowledge them, repent, and keep on fighting with our child or children. This will teach our youth that they will never be perfect but should always press toward the mark of spiritual maturity.

Serve in the youth ministry. Finally, I want to also say that when parents serve in the youth ministry it leads to stronger spiritual development for the entire family. Some parents can serve weekly, some can serve twice per month or once per month, but frequent service in the youth ministry is good for the parents of youth and the youth. Only parents serving in youth ministry ought to give their child space and not use it as an opportunity to press or pressure their children among their peers. I cannot say this enough, youth ministry needs the involvement of parents in order to succeed. Youth pastors have to work closely with the parents of their youth. There are ways to serve youth directly and ways to serve them indirectly, but I recommend a parent who have youth in youth ministries to at least serve once or twice, if not per month, then do it per year. This way you can have a better understanding of what is happening with your child and whether working directly with youth is something you can see yourself doing. Youth workers need parents to be involved, and parents need youth workers to serve their youth.

TO THE YOUTH WORKERS

To those in the congregation who are volunteers or staff in a youth ministry, the main role should be to support and follow the vision of the youth pastor by faithfully serving the youth. Those who serve the youth through ministry programming and discipleship can support the needs of the youth in our congregations. Supporting the youth pastor and/or director of youth ministry can increase the perceived value of young believers in your church. Below are three ways you can increase the value of the youth you serve.

Pray for the youth. Youth workers should pray for the youth regularly. When we pray for our youth, God has a way of drawing our hearts toward them. They become more valuable to us. The truth is what we see physically is often a result of our prayer time spiritually. Youth ministry is not natural but spiritual work. The devil and demonic forces are at work to destroy the lives of young people, and spiritual warfare is necessary in youth ministry.

Additionally, we need to pray for the spiritual development of our youth. Prayer can do much more than anything else we do. Prayer reveals to God that we recognize our need for him. Prayer invites God in, to do what we cannot do without him. Prayer also strengthens us and provides the grace for our perseverance. In addition to the youth, we need youth workers to pray for the youth pastor and other youth workers. Youth ministers are under more attack than we care to know, and they are carrying more weight than we can understand. Youth workers are the right and left hand of the youth pastor God has put in place for such a time as this. It is a vital necessity to pray for God's leader behind it all. Prayer is a huge key to everything. If we plead for our youth, we will not have to plead to them.

Know the youth. It is important for youth workers to get to know the youth they serve. When we get to know the youth personally, their value automatically increases in our eyes. Learning the names of youth is important. One of the reasons a street-involved young man like myself would give any attention to the church is simply because the youth pastor remembered my name. When you know youth by name and get to spend time with them in different settings, building relationships with them, it helps with the influence and work of development in their lives. Sometimes writing names down and praying for those names all week can help you to know them before you really know them.

Nurture the youth. By nurture the youth, I mean we need youth workers to help them to grow and spend time developing their understanding of God and their walk in Christ. Just like prayer and building relationships with youth, nurturing them increases their value in your life as well. In chapter seven, an entire chapter was dedicated to the important need of discipleship in youth ministry. However, there does not need to be a formal discipleship class for you to disciple and nurture teenagers. Youth workers can disciple young people while playing video games with them or by playing chess, cards, or board games. Youth workers do not have to set up a biblical counseling meeting with youth in order to provide spiritual direction for them. All that is needed to be done is to be there in their life and speak into it as opportunity avails itself. Subtle and non-formal discipleship is often more impactful.

PARENTING THE YOUTH

As this chapter concludes, I want to make it clear that not all parents have biological children and not all biological parents are able to be there for their children. There are cases where youth need members of the congregation to be pseudo-parental support in their lives. This is a very important way a congregation of God and especially youth workers can help support youth. Often in the urban context, as well as many other contexts, parents are not around. Whether due to sickness, death, incarceration, or addiction, some youth need extra parental support. The fact is some youth need for members of the church to become step-parents. This means we need men and women from the congregation to step into the lives of youth at the church to be parental figures to them in their season of adolescence. Youth workers who are around the youth the most should be first in line.

You do not have to have a child to be a parent, and some are able to be a parent to more than just their own biological children. The youth workers and others in the congregation should play a role in guiding and supporting youth, and the leadership of the church should convey when that role is needed. Parenting youth requires dedication, labor, and collaboration. It also takes the combined effort of an entire congregation to help youth thrive as they grow into adulthood. When the parents and the youth ministry work together in partnership to develop spiritually mature youth, everybody wins. In the body of Christ, everyone has a gift, everyone plays a role for the edification of the entire body. Parents, youth workers, lay leaders, and the entire congregation all have a role to play in the lives of our youth. This responsibility refers to the ministers and leaders of the congregation as well.

A DEEPER DIVE

The following communications are intended for reflection on ways your entire congregation can value, contribute, and support the ministry work of youth.

1. As a member of the body of Christ, can you identify ways to contribute to the well-being of the youth and youth ministry at your church?

2. As a parent of a teenager, or parents who have raised teenagers, reflect on some ways that you can collaborate with the youth leaders (i.e., youth ministers, youth workers) to aid the spiritual growth and support of your teenagers?

3. As a single parent of a teenager or multiple teenagers, write down a few ways that the church could better assist you with your child's/children's participation in youth ministry programming. Communicate your ideas with the youth leaders at your church.

4. As members of the congregation with no children or adult children, reflect on ways that you can support the youth ministry or parents of teenagers at the church.

10

TO THE MINISTERS OF THE CONGREGATION

Even to the shepherds, Thus says the Lord GOD:
Ah, shepherds of Israel who have been feeding
yourselves! Should not shepherds feed the sheep?

EZEKIEL 34:2 ESV

THE MINISTERS OF THE CONGREGATION are God's gift to the body of Christ and the assembly of his people. Paul lets us know that God "gave *the apostles, the prophets, the evangelists, the pastors* and *teachers* to equip his people for works of service, so that the body of Christ may be built up" (Ephesians 4:11-12, emphasis mine). Our churches have elders, ministers, pastors, bishops, and overseers so that members, including youth, can be equipped to do the work of the ministry to strengthen the entire congregation. However, many ministers in a congregation are only sensitive to the needs of the adult members.

If the truth be told, sometimes pastors focus on the adults because they are tithing contributors to the ministry and help to keep the church going. We usually don't see the youth as vital contributors in that way, but to think this way is to despise our youth. This type of thinking is a church-incorporated approach to shepherding. The fact is ministers serve as shepherds responsible for leading, feeding, and protecting the sheep, especially the younger and most vulnerable in the pact. This chapter is written as a reminder and encouragement to the spiritual ministerial leaders in our congregations to not forget about their responsibility of making sure the youth in the congregation are being fed as well.

In Ezekiel 34, the prophet is speaking on behalf of God and rebuking the shepherds of Israel for their selfishness. The shepherds, who were in positions of authority at the time, were misleading the people of God and taking care of their own personal needs instead of the needs of God's people. They were clothing and feeding themselves well while scattering the sheep of Israel to become food and prey to the wild beasts. The point of the passage is that God is going to hold the shepherds who are the ministerial leaders of Israel responsible for this death and devastation because rather than caring for the flock they cared only for themselves.

GOD CARES FOR THE YOUTH

God's rebuke in Ezekiel 34 is to be understood as his care for his people who were being hurt by the selfish actions of their shepherds. When our leadership is focused only on the things we see as important rather than what God says is important, it becomes selfish leadership. Today I know that pastors and ministers out here are not intentionally turning their backs on the youth and refusing to focus on the things young people need in the church. However, when we are led by our hearts and our own desires rather than the Scriptures, this is exactly what can happen. We can neglect other parts of the ministry, including the youth. One of the challenges of pastoring is constantly seeing things that need to be addressed in the congregation but not being able to do anything about it. As gifted as ministers are, they may be able to do anything, but they cannot do everything. Pastors need their congregations to help them stay on top of the things needed for their youth.

Neglect of youth focus is usually not intentional, but when we who are pastors become self-absorbed in our initiatives and blinded by the constant needs of the church that are fighting for our attention, neglect and selfish tunnel vision leads to the hurt of our youth who are being abandoned. Jesus spoke up for children and made it clear that they were a priority for him. As leaders, we must care about the things that God cares about as well. In our churches, we have both ministers who serve primarily adults and those who serve primarily youth, and I would first like to encourage those who serve the youth.

TO THE YOUTH MINISTERS

To the youth minister, I have been in your shoes and understand the tremendous weight you carry. Besides the senior pastorate, I believe the youth ministry can be the largest and heaviest ministry burden in the church. I know that all youth ministers may not be considered pastors, but all pastors are considered ministers. It ought to be an honor to serve as a youth minister. In a sense, the youth pastorate is like a micro-version of the senior pastorate. Youth ministers are shepherding the lives of the youth and those who work with them.

Many youth ministers have to prep and preach sermons every week, leading, feeding, caring, protecting the flock, budgeting, addressing issues, and serving well. The youth need ministers to address their unique needs, and God is depending on his ministers to faithfully live into their calling to raise up mature Christian teenagers. It is so crucially important that youth ministers do not rush their season. Sometimes our passion to become a senior pastor can get in the way of God preparing us for that call. We must watch and wait on God. A major challenge among youth pastors in our urban churches is not sticking around long enough to bear lasting fruit. Youth ministers coming into a youth ministry ought not leave the ministry worse off than it was when they first received it. The ministry should always grow and become better before we pass the baton to someone else.

To youth ministers who may be thinking they are missing out on better ministry opportunities, it is important to know that ministry is not about us. It is about how God has called us and where he has sent us to serve. There is no better place to be than where God has called you to be. For youth ministry, the minister's role is vital. When there is no longevity in the lead youth minister, it can bring about confusion in the youth ministry, which usually leads to a decline in the functioning of the youth church.

It is really important that young ministers not despise ministry among the youth. God blesses ministers in the next season, based on their faithfulness in the season of the previous call. Youth ministry has a great benefit for youth ministers and the youth they serve. I served youth for over twenty years, and my last youth pastor call ended when I was forty-two years old. I had no shame about it, and I loved it to the core. I knew it was time to leave because my heart was turning toward other issues, my patience and tolerance for the young and especially issues of the young was decreasing, and God was pressing other issues on my heart around the church as a whole. God had released me to pursue a full-time senior pastor role. I served youth from my early twenties into my early forties, and God has blessed me for my faithfulness. I learned more about how to shepherd a church and pastoral ministry in the context of leading the youth ministry than I have in any other way, including seminary.

Senior pastoral ministry is nothing to rush into and patience is a godly virtue. We may see colleagues move into seemingly more prominent ministry positions and roles and may desire to move into something ourselves, but we have to be led by God and not our personal preferences. I know how people in the ministry can treat youth ministers as youngsters or minimize what they do. Not only can youth and youth ministry be despised, but the youth pastor can also be despised. But let me remind youth pastors that we serve and perform for an audience of only one, or should I say three-in-one, the Triune God. God's minister must always be confident in their abilities and calling as ministers and seek to please no one but God. In my season of youth ministry, I knew my time to move into other areas of ministry would come when and if God led me there. We should seek calling not opportunities because the devil can give us opportunities, but God gives a calling. Below are a few reflections for youth pastors or ministers looking to become youth pastors.

Discerning youth ministry. If you are looking to become a youth pastor, my prayer is that you discern your calling in at least three ways. First, discern your passion: Are you passionate about youth and youth ministry? Second, discern your gifts:

Are you good at serving and working with youth and adults on the team? Does God greatly use you in efforts to minister to adolescents? Third, discern your calling to serve youth. Often when we start a ministry assignment, we start with what we want to do. This is passion, and passion is but part of the process. We also need to discern our gifts and our calling.

Discerning a call usually begins with an internal sense that God is leading us to do something, like feeling God's push to serve young people. However, discerning a call should not end there. It is important to determine whether other people see the calling of God on our lives. After feeling God's call and having it affirmed by others, then there is a good chance that God is calling one to serve youth. If God is calling you, you are gifted to serve youth, and you are passionate about serving youth, then there has been affirmation on three levels, and it would make sense to move forward with a commitment to serve young people for the long haul.

Longevity is important. Youth ministry is not for the faint of heart. It can be challenging and become hard to bear, but if we are called, we have to be faithful. Cultivating a thriving youth ministry takes time, and taking time is very important. To the youth ministers, I encourage you to love, serve, and commit to remain with your young people until God says differently. Any youth pastor in service for less than three or four years will most likely be unable to set a spiritually fruitful culture that will last once they are gone. The most successful youth ministries I have observed in urban youth ministry have youth pastors who have served ten years or more.[1] This is not to say that every youth minister should serve this long but to point out the fact that longevity matters.

Keep the youth visible. In addition to the fight to stay with our youth is the fight to make sure the youth are seen and have what they need. When I served as youth pastor at Oakdale Covenant Church, Dr. Griffin often reminded me that the squeaky wheel gets the oil. In other words, if I am not making him aware of the needs and the issues surrounding the youth, then they most likely will remain unaddressed. This is why when I had opportunities to preach to the adults, I made sure they heard what was going on with the youth. I made sure that our youth were seen, and in order to be seen, I had to make them visible to the adult congregation.

I made sure I shared testimonies about what God was doing with the youth and allowed youth to share their testimonies with the congregation as often as possible. I fought for opportunities for the youth to speak, minister, testify, or share in adult and special church-wide services. I used bulletin boards to post pictures every month of what the youth were doing. No adult in the church could pass by without noticing what God was doing with the teenagers. We had a strong social media presence and a physical presence to make sure the adults continued to see and think about the youth all the time. At staff meetings we fought for what the youth needed. If they needed a space of their own, it was our job to fight for it and help figure it out. The senior pastor can help us to do the problem solving, but this will not happen until we make the issue visible.

The youth minister's battlefield. The life of a youth minister is a battlefield. Youth ministers must fight for time to study and go to war to protect the sermon prep time. Youth ministers must not water down or become lazy with their sermons. The better your preaching and teaching the stronger your youth and workers will become. Youth ministers must discern where their youth are and what the youth need if they are going to learn and address those issues their generation is up against. Youth ministers have to fight for their own holiness and spiritual purity. Personal holiness cannot be over-emphasized. The power is not of ourselves—the power comes in our connectedness to God. Our holiness will be key to the fruitfulness of the ministry. God will not bless those who are not right with him. We cannot be a sinful mess and lead a spiritually strong youth ministry. There is a battle for holiness and purity. This goes for both male and female youth ministers.

Youth minister's duties. Finally, as the youth minister, pastor, and overseer of the souls of teenagers, there are six primary duties you will need to focus on doing well: reaching, teaching, preaching, caring, protecting, and leading. Our first duty is to reach the youth. Youth ministers have to focus on reaching youth in the community and the church. Youth ministers have to minister on both sides of the cross. This means constantly looking to reach lost youth outside of the church with the gospel as we are faithfully discipling Christian youth inside the church.

The next duty is to feed the youth. Youth ministers must faithfully feed their flock. We have to study hard, construct and deliver impactful transforming messages, and teach Bible lessons consistently and faithfully, always having done adequate preparation. We have to feed young people corporately and individually as we mentor and disciple them.

Along with teaching and preaching to feed our youth, the youth pastor's next responsibility is to care for the youth. When they are struggling, be there. When they are sick, we check on them. When they are depressed, we must be present. When they get into trouble, we have to help them. We should be asking questions about their spiritual walk whenever we can. These are a few ways not only to care for them but to show them that we care. Because youth do not care about how much we know until they know how much we care.

The next important duty of the youth minister is to protect the youth. We have to protect the youth who are growing from the youth who are distracting them. We must go to war to protect them from the challenges we see in the community, and from false teaching, especially some of the unique false religions that are spreading in urban African American areas and other communities of color. Many Afrocentric religions such as the Black Hebrew Israelites, Five Percenter Islam, the Nation of Islam, and the Moors could be seen as using issues around Black identity and nationalism to draw our teenagers into their false religions. We have to protect the youth by teaching and explaining truth from error and by equipping them to do the same. It is the youth minister's duty to help them to filter sound doctrine from error on social media and internet platforms. Yes, I know this is truly a lot. Being a youth minister in urban and African American settings is a burden and a call that has to be taken seriously. But if God has called you, know that his yoke is easy and his burden is light. For those who accept this call of the Lord, please know that God will renew your strength as you serve him.

The final duty is that the youth minister must lead their young people. A shepherd's job is to lead their flock. We must be sure to lead not only in word but in our deeds. Youth can follow what we say better when they see what we do. Teenagers are more likely to do what they see us do than they are to do what they hear us say. Youth ministers have to practice what they preach. Living out the faith and communicating the faith is a powerful track for our youth to take flight. Leading young people to be all that God is calling them to be is a journey of biblical exploration and spiritual practice. I encourage youth ministers to war and fight to stick with the call and live up to the calling by God's grace.

TO THE SENIOR PASTOR

As I conclude this chapter and book, I want to encourage senior pastors. Youth ministry is a ministry that most and not only urban churches are struggling with. If you are a senior pastor in the urban context, chances are you have a struggling youth ministry, a youth ministry that has declined, or a youth ministry in need of a youth director or a youth pastor. You are not alone. Churches in many other ethnic areas and demographic contexts are also struggling to provide a thriving youth ministry. The turnover rate of youth pastors, the complaints of adults for more to be provided for their teens, and the challenge to develop a sufficient budget to address the growing needs of young people are all real pressing issues in our churches.

This is the experience of many lead pastors in urban and African American churches. These pressing issues exist as there are dozens of other important issues for the senior pastor to manage. I know this is tough, but this is also the call of a senior pastor. The church is multigenerational, and the youth need just as much ministry attention as everyone else. This is why we must seek God's wisdom and guidance for a unique plan to address the needs of youth in our congregations. The senior pastor of the church can support and fight for the needs of youth and their leaders to increase the perceived value of young believers in the congregation. I would like to leave with you some principles that will help with seeing the value and potential of youth ministry at your church.

Youth ministry strengthens and grows a church. As a senior pastor who grew into adulthood through youth ministry, I witnessed the supernatural, spiritual, and numeric growth of a church that invested in their youth. In about ten years, the youth ministry grew from about twenty youth in weekly worship to over 1,500 youth in weekly worship, and many of these youth contributed to practical ministry at this church. Many of these youth returned after attending college to serve as adults and many went to school in the city because they did not want to leave their church. In the transition of the young generation to the adult generation, these youth became serious adult Christians who are still giving their time, talents, and treasures to the ministry of the church today and now have their own children experiencing ministry as youth in the same congregation.

This youth ministry contributed greatly to the spiritual and numeric growth of the congregation, which at that same time grew from about 200 members to over 25,000 members in ten years. The church took care of the youth, and the youth took care of the church. In fact, at the Salem Baptist Church of Chicago, my colleague and friend Dr. Charlie Dates, who was once a teen at Salem's Christian Academy, another ministry for youth under the umbrella of the Salem Baptist Church of Chicago, became the senior pastor of the church that nurtured him as a youth. Youth ministry matters, and when done well, the entire church will benefit from it. Nothing just happens, and nothing happens overnight. It takes time to raise youth into mature Christians, but it is worth the time and effort that it takes.

Time, not money. After being a senior pastor for ten years, I have been in spaces with colleagues struggling for a way to fund youth ministry. Many pastors even cut their youth ministry because they feel like the funds are not there. However, we must remember that our call is to the ministry of the entire church and not just the adults. As previously mentioned, the fact is whether consciously or subconsciously, many pastors choose to fund adult ministry because they perceive the adults as able to give funding back to the church. But it is important to understand that it is not always about money. I have colleagues in more affluent contexts who have more than enough funding and have more staff for their youth ministry than many in the urban context have for their entire church, but they are still struggling with their youth ministries.

Unfortunately, youth are often seen as unemployed and non-contributors economically to the church, but this is not the truth as I will explain shortly. Other pastors look at the pressing needs of their congregations and determine they cannot afford to do full-time youth ministry, but I say that our churches cannot afford not to do youth ministry. Every church needs funding to do ministry, but the most important need for youth are godly people who have a heart for them and who are committed to serving them. In the urban context, there is usually more time than money available, but the good news is that what is needed most is time, not financing. Youth ministry is crucial to the future of any church. I know that it is more about the time that we put into the ministry than it is about the funding we put into it.

Youth bring parents. As I stated before, I want to share more about the myth of youth not contributing financially to the church. It is helpful for senior pastors to look at funding youth ministry as an investment that will bear future fruit. There is usually a return on the investments we make in our youth. Youth who are spiritually developing will draw their parents to our churches. When parents see the spiritual development of their children along with their commitment and consistent involvement in our churches, these parents will eventually come to see what the church is all about. It will be important to have a plan of action to connect and draw these parents in deeper. Investing time into youth ministry usually leads to families growing and becoming believers who become contributing members of our churches.

Parents will bring funding, service, gifts, and other contributions to our churches that their children can't (in their youth season). While youth are typically able to contribute less fiscally to the congregation, when their parents are drawn to the church, it helps to produce more resources for the ministry to do more ministry. Youth who are developed into Christians represent the next generation of parents who will not only attend church but make sure their children who represent the next generation attend as well. With parents committed to giving the necessary time and commitment to young people in our congregations and community, our youth ministries can thrive while helping the church to excel.

Hire for heart more than experience. Finally, as a pastor hiring a youth minister or director for youth ministry, it will be important to hire someone who has the right heart, even if they do not have a lot of experience. Learning youth ministry leadership is easier than trying to use someone with experience who has no heart or passion for the youth. As we hire people with a heart for youth, we should make sure we are hiring for the youth and not ourselves. When I say hire for the youth and not for ourselves as senior pastors, what I mean is we have to be careful not to factor in all of the particular needs of the church when hiring for the youth. If we want the youth ministry to thrive, we should primarily factor in the needs of the youth not the congregation as a whole.

Too often we stretch our youth leaders too thin because we are blinded by all of the needs of the church. For example, when we hire a youth pastor to serve youth and also help with several of the adult responsibilities of the church, it can often impede upon their ability to do well with the youth. We do not want a youth minister who can do a lot of things adequately but nothing well. We should want youth ministers who can do youth ministry well with our youth. This does not mean we want to hire a youth minister who will never preach to the adults because preaching to the adults helps to inform them about the youth and their responsibility to youth, which helps draw more youth workers and garner support for the youth ministry. However, senior pastors have to be careful about overworking youth ministers in other areas of the church because the growth of our young people is an investment in the growth of the entire congregation. This is not microwave ministry but crock pot ministry. Slow and steady will win the race.

Applicants for youth ministers who have impressive resumes should be examined to see whether they have a heart and passion for youth. This is really important. Not only do the youth need to see and feel the minister's passion for them, but the congregation needs to see and feel the youth minister's passion for their children. Even more than this, we have to look for language in their applications and/or resumes of a calling to serve youth. When you are a senior pastor, depending on where your church is in its journey, it can be difficult to hire people who require development, but often it is required to develop them. Sometimes we have to hire people who need development because their vision, heart, and calling are very clear.

However, when hiring them we should not leave them to fend for themselves. They have to be nurtured and discipled and developed as ministry leaders to our youth. This may require some of the senior pastor's time or extra time from other capable ministers on the church roster. The bottom line is that sometimes the senior pastor has to fight to ensure that the youth minister is mentored and developed into the leader they need to be. It is also important to understand that this mentorship will not last forever. A year or two at best would be enough to get the ball rolling.

Your youth deserve the best, and as the senior leader of your congregation, you will want to set your youth ministry up for success. Remember the seeds you sow will grow underneath the surface where it is not visible long before the fruit can be noticeable above the soil. Senior pastors who do not despise or underestimate their youth are committed to providing what they need to develop into faithful followers of Christ. Ministers in our congregations play a vital role in supporting the youth and leading the congregation to do the same. God cares for the youth and is looking for shepherds who not only feed themselves but also the flock of which youth are a part. Whether youth minister, associate minister, or senior pastor, we all play a very important role in the ministry to and through teenagers in our congregations. We need our ministers to value our youth in word and practice as we lead our congregations to do the same, and we need the entire congregation to get involved on some level with ensuring that there is ministry focus on the youth in the congregation.

A DEEPER DIVE

The following communications are intended for ministerial leaders in the church for reflection in order to help lead, feed, care, and protect the teenagers and their ministry in the church.

1. As a minister of the church serving primarily in adult ministry, how can you contribute to the work and well-being of youth ministry?

2. As a youth minister, identify the most challenging obstacles you face in serving the youth.

3. As a senior pastor, identify the most challenging obstacles you face in the development and support of the youth ministry.

4. In what ways can you see the growth of the youth ministry contributing to the growth of the church as a whole?

Conclusion

NECESSARY MINISTRY

YOUTH MINISTRY IS NECESSARY. It should not be approached as a luxury our churches can do without. The traumatrigenic communities that are impacting the lives of urban inner city youth require extra support beyond the family for the work of prevention and intervention and sometimes reentry from the challenges they are facing. There is a felt need for an expansion of robust youth ministry in urban and African American communities that is necessary to address this growing trauma and chaos among the urban youth population. The despising of youth, whether in the streets or in the church, leads to less support for them because their value and potential to us are underestimated or unseen altogether. This also contributes to the crisis of youth ministry in many urban cities across the United States, and the hope of restoring the worth of youth is in the church. This is why we must not despise our youth but raise them up to do what they are uniquely gifted and designed to do—be young urban missionaries among their peers.

I believe that the work of youth ministry is paramount to addressing the unique needs young people are facing throughout the urban centers of North America. Young people are unique, receptive, and often easily persuaded, which means providing the right influences around them are key to their proper development. Youth will be influenced to become who they will develop into whether by the impact of their worlds or the influences of our churches. If our churches are not serious about investing in and influencing young people for Christ, believe me, this world will invest in them and lead them according to the ways of the world.

We are in need of strong youth ministries in our congregations to be a bridge in the life of urban teenagers looking to persevere through the drama of their environment. The gospel of Jesus Christ still saves and when we understand the potential of our youth to bring hope, change, and reconciliation to their peers, we can't help but make contributions to equip them for that work. As we understand youth ministry as youth doing ministry and not doing ministry to youth, they become the vessels of God and we become a support to their work in the church and the community.

The state of urban youth ministry has declined from where it once was for various reasons, but the church of Jesus Christ has to uplift and magnify this work of God in and through youth in order to help raise youth ministry's value in the eyes of our congregations. Restoring the value of urban youth ministry is crucial. Though younger than most of our congregations they must be seen as believers, not babies. They can contribute, they can be discipled, and they can serve God and his congregation with the support of our churches. In this book I have shared many stories that arose from youth ministry in very dark, difficult, and real urban inner-city contexts. Some stories were about my years as a youth, some were about youth ministries that I served as a youth leader, and later as a pastor, but all of the stories are very real and reveal to us that youth can make great contributions if we commit the time and service to them.

I cannot over stress the necessity of youth being valued, evangelized, discipled, and fought for in our congregations. We never know who God is raising up among us, but in this season of life, they will need the entire body of Christ to contribute to what God is doing in their lives. Their parents, congregation, and the ministers in the congregation must collaborate in the development of young soldiers for Christ. We cannot be like the ancient Israelites in the generation of David who despised David on every side. His father, siblings, king, and enemies all despised him, counted him out, and saw no potential in him—but God was on his side. Youth who are not ashamed of their relationship with God, are well versed in the Word of God, and fearless in the ministry of the Lord will bring fruit and development to our entire congregation. Youth are not always easy to work with, and some of their challenges are not for the faint of heart, but love will cover a multitude of sin. The more we love our youth, the more the youth will express their love in the world based on how they have been loved by us.

If we are going to help youth in our cities, we must address the youth ministry crisis, which starts with our recognition of their value in the kingdom of God. This work has been a clear call to action in our churches. Our youth are in need of our investments. They are in need of mentors, directors, pastors, and leaders who will put in the time and commitment to help them become who God is calling them to be. Our youth need to know who they are in God and what they can accomplish in the kingdom, but in order for all of this to be brought into existence, we must not despise them. We can value youth and support youth without being a hands-on youth ministry worker, and we can serve youth if we have experienced the grace of God in youth ministry or our life as a youth. What youth need is our time more than anything, and I know that what we sow into their lives is what we will reap.

This book was written as a testimonial to the fact that God still raises up strong Christian youth, and he is still using the young, least likely, and least expected to accomplish great feats for his kingdom. This work aims to convince the church not to underestimate its teenagers. It is my desire for youth not to be counted out because they are younger. This work is a call to the entire church to expect greatness from our young people and to equip and support their work in the kingdom. This is the only way they will not be despised. Churches that value young people invest in them. They invest time, they invest funding, they invest resources, and they expect greatness as a result of the investments. I pray that every reader will be able to see what God has done and continues to do through young people and envision his grace upon our youth.

Youth ministry is a necessary work that should be taken seriously in all of our Christian churches. Whether urban, suburban, rural, or otherwise, our youth are important. They are powerful, they are capable, and most importantly, they are our future. I pray that those reading this book will help to advocate for young people in their churches, participate in youth programming, and support ministry to and through youth whenever possible. Our future is in the hands of our youth and the future of our youth is in our hands. May God be with us all as we work to bring value to our young people and hope to our cities by the grace of God.

ACKNOWLEDGMENTS

THIS BOOK WOULD NOT HAVE BEEN WRITTEN without the continued support of my wife, Vernée. She is my true partner in ministry, and her support means everything. To InterVarsity Press (IVP) for the opportunity to share my heart and personal stories for inspiration to the church. I also would like to acknowledge the help of my editor at IVP, Nilwona Nowlin, for her guidance and care in the process of completing this work and helping it to be a great resource for youth ministries, especially in the urban and African American setting. I am also very grateful for the entire editorial team at IVP for your hard work and commitment to get this work out to the world. Your collaborative effort has made a tremendous difference.

To my mentors in pastoral, urban, and youth ministry, Dr. James T. Meeks, Dr. John Teter, Pastor Harvey F. Carey, and Dr. D. Darrell Griffin, I am eternally grateful for the wisdom, guidance, and investments you have contributed to my life as a youth, youth pastor, and urban lead pastor. What I have learned and experienced in the joy of youth ministry shared in this book is a result of the time and attention you have given me over the years.

To our ministry family at Kingdom Covenant Church Chicago, thank you for ten years of service as your pastor and the support you give to projects like this book, to the support you give to the children and youth of our congregation, and for your commitment to evangelize, equip, and empower people for the kingdom of God. I have grown under your care and support, and much of what I am able to do is because of your encouragement and assistance.

To the youth in the cities and congregations across America, you are my inspiration; you are fearfully and wonderfully made. I acknowledge your worth, potential, and our need for your contributions. This mighty, creative, and influential generation is the inspiration for this book and the hope for our future.

Finally, thank you to the one true God, my Lord and Savior Jesus Christ who pulled me out of the depths of urban decay and like a potter put my life back together again. I am forever grateful, forever in love, and my life is forever dedicated to you.

KEY TERMS

Black(s): Means the same as African American and used interchangeably with African American

Black churches: Congregations that are predominantly African American and within predominantly African American communities

Busters: A derogatory slang term used to describe someone who is seen as weak in the urban streets

Crash-and-grab thefts: When thieves use a vehicle to crash into a store or place of business in order to steal supplies, typically in large quantities

Drinking lean: Slang for a drink, usually soda or juice, mixed with over-the-counter drugs that contain codeine ("lean"), like cough syrup, for getting high

Gang banging: Slang word used to describe the active gang activities of a person or people who are gang members

Gangster Disciple Nation: An African American street gang that started in Chicago in the 1960s but has since spread to major cities across the United States and abroad

Homie (Home boy): Slang word used in urban inner cities to describe very close friends

The Hood: Short for neighborhood; a slang term used for an urban African American inhabited neighborhood predominantly of low economic status

In the streets: Describes a person or persons living according to the unwritten codes of life in an urban low-income community

Jumping/to jump: When multiple people ban together in order to outnumber, attack, and beat someone

Kingdom: Short for Kingdom Covenant Church Chicago

The Kingdom: Short for the kingdom of God

Lame(s): A derogatory slang word typically used to describe someone who is not cool, respected, or accepted in the streets; also used by gang members to describe people who are civilians or non-gang members

Ride or die: Slang word that means loyalty to someone or something no matter what

RIP: Acronym for rest in peace, means deceased

Snatched (off the streets): Slang term for kidnapping, usually for ransom

The Set: An area in a gang community that a particular faction of the gang is identified with.

Swagger: A slang word used to describe the style and urban persona, sometimes called *swag* in short

Urban: Densely populated low-income areas

Urban churches: Churches in densely populated low-income areas

Urban youth ministry: Ministry to and through teenagers in urban communities

Youth church: Youth's equivalent of Sunday service; church designed for teenagers (also includes middle schoolers in some churches)

Youth workers: Adults who work in youth groups or youth ministries in the church

Wild Wild Hundreds: A low-income urban populated area on the far south side of Chicago where territories are labeled by street numbers that are in the hundreds (100th street, 115th street, 130th street, etc.)

NOTES

1 A CULTURAL DISCLAIMER

[1]Phil Jackson, "Jesus on the Mic: The Hip Hop Church," in *A Heart for the Community: New Models for Urban and Suburban Ministry*, eds. John E. Fueder and Noel Castellanos (Chicago: Moody Publishers, 2009), 166.

2 LIFE OR DEATH CIRCUMSTANCES

[1]Dave Wright, "A Brief History of Youth Ministry," *The Gospel Coalition*, April 2, 2012, www.thegospelcoalition.org/article/a-brief-history-of-youth-ministry/.

[2]Aaron Earls, "The Next Generation Is Leaving the Faith Earlier Than You Realize," Lifeway Research, October 4, 2023, https://research.lifeway.com/2023/10/04/the-next-generation-is-leaving-the-faith-earlier-than-you-realize/.

[3]"Youth Pastor Demographics and Statistics in the US," Zippia, accessed April 5, 2024, www.zippia.com/youth-pastor-jobs/demographics/.

[4]Jared Kennedy, "Where Did Youth Ministry Go Wrong? Identifying a Way Forward," Crossway, June 22, 2022, www.crossway.org/articles/where-did-youth-ministry-go-wrong-identifying-a-way-forward/.

[5]Allison Fletcher Acosta et al., "And the Youth Shall Lead Us: Stories of Young People on the Frontlines of U.S. Social Movements," Civil Rights Teaching, accessed October 22, 2024, www.civilrightsteaching.org/resource/youth-shall-lead-us.

[6]Acosta et al., "And the Youth Shall Lead Us."

[7]Kennedy, "Where Did Youth Ministry Go Wrong?"

3 DON'T DESPISE OUR YOUTH

[1]William Danker, ed., *A Greek—English Lexicon of the New Testament and Other Early Christian Literature*, 3rd ed. (Chicago: The University of Chicago Press, 2000), 529.

[2]The bar/bat mitzvah is a centuries-old ceremony for the rite of passage that marks the transition of Jewish boys and girls into adulthood.

4 DEFINING YOUTH MINISTRY

[1]Encyclopedia.com, "Children, Youth Ministries," accessed November 1, 2024, www.encyclopedia.com/children/encyclopedias-almanacs -transcripts-and-maps/youth-ministries.

[2]Encyclopedia.com, "Children, Youth Ministries."

[3]Jared Kennedy, "Where Did Youth Ministry Go Wrong? Identifying a Way Forward," Crossway, June 22, 2022, www.crossway.org/articles /where-did-youth-ministry-go-wrong-identifying-a-way-forward/.

[4]*Shema* is a Hebrew word that means "to hear or listen." This was a central prayer of confession for those of the Jewish faith based on Deuteronomy 6:4, which begins with the word *shema*.

8 THE LANGUAGE OF LOVE

[1]Gary Chapman, *The 5 Love Languages: The Secret to Love That Lasts*, reprint edition (Chicago: Northfield Publishing, 2017).

[2]GDA Speakers, "Gary Chapman," Gdaspeakers.com, accessed November 26, 2024, www.gdaspeakers.com/speaker/gary-chapman/.

[3]For those who would like to know more about spiritual gifts, you can go to www.5lovelanguages.com and/or take the Love Language Quiz at https://5lovelanguages.com/quizzes/love-language.

9 TO THE CONGREGATION

[1]*America Undercover*, "Gang War: Bangin' In Little Rock," HBO, directed by Marc Levin, aired August 2, 1994.

10 TO THE MINISTERS OF THE CONGREGATION

[1]Among the youth pastors in the Chicago area are Harvey F. Carey (Salem Baptist Church of Chicago), John F. Hannah (St. James Church of God in Christ), Titus Lee (South Side Tabernacle), and Phil Jackson (Lawndale Community Church).

Like this book?

Scan the code to discover more content like this!

Get on IVP's email list to receive special offers, exclusive book news, and thoughtful content from your favorite authors on topics you care about.

ĩvp | InterVarsity Press